Getting into a Good College May Not Be as Hard as You Think

An Eight-Step Guide For Parents To Help Kids Get Good Grades And Accepted Into A Good College

David Hoy PhD

For Sandy, My love and Inspiration, Always and Forever

Table of Contents

Introduction

"You are the bows from which your children as living arrows are sent forth."
— Kahlil Gibran

I sat in my den this morning enjoying my first few coveted sips of coffee and reading the most recent *Special Edition of Time Magazine*. The entire focus was on mental health. There were two sections I was particularly interested in: *"The Loneliness Epidemic"* and *"Depression on Campus."* As I read, I reflected on the decades I have spent working with families and teens. My mind was barraged with video-like moving images of client stories that are permanently etched in my memory; not only my personal clients, but also hundreds of others who have been seen by colleagues in my offices. Although it was painful to read that loneliness and mental health struggles have reached alarming levels, not just in the US, but all over the world, I am happy to see the discussion brought above ground and shared with the masses. The reality is that there is an epidemic, and we are now aware that loneliness, depression, and anxiety have become serious public health problems that lead to disease, lower mortality rates, and struggles at home and in school. What's more, it is our kids who are the most affected. College campuses are overwhelmed with students seeking mental health services, however, they are a long way from being able to meet such demands. Do you know what it takes for a teen to ask for help with anything, let alone with mental health? Teens are not wired this way, and the fact that they are coming forward *en masse* on college campuses means they are in crisis. Last year I interviewed 50 college students and recent graduates to get their perspectives on teen mental health. "Is everything we are hearing in the news about the mental health crisis on college campuses true?" Their answer was a resounding "YES." We discussed the utility of mentoring programs on campuses and I asked them if mentoring programs needed to mask the topic of mental health due to a stigma that may deter kids from engaging. "NO," they replied. "Everyone knows about it." Their responses made me wonder whether the stigma around mental health is more prevalent with us grown-ups than our children. I had to ask the students and graduates about their use of electronics and social media. We hear stories daily in the news about the negative impact of the internet, cell phones, and social media on mental health. They not only shared stories of friends and acquaintances on campuses, but also some of their own struggles with electronics and social media. In chapter 6, I discuss and provide strong evidence linking electronics, cell phones, and social media with increases in mental health problems, suicide rates, and problems on college campuses.

I can imagine that it must be daunting to think about your child's struggles in school or with mental health as a large social problem. That's why I am here. I feel fortunate to be at a place in my career where I can assist on a broad social level, and am called to do so as a health activist. This book is intended as a coaching guide for parents to help kids succeed in school and get into good colleges. My goal is to empower you with information, not only to provide context but also give you actionable solutions to help your child overcome their barriers to school success. I have been advised against presenting too much research and getting too "teachy" in this non-fiction self-help book. However, I feel it's important to show you the big picture when it comes to the overall problems and solutions. In this book, I have used research, personal experience, and hypothetical stories as examples in a very conversational style that I believe will be most helpful for you. As I relate client stories, I have altered names and other identifying information in order to protect confidentiality.

How did I get here? I have a blended background in the fields of psychology, education, coaching, and physical fitness. I started a private counseling, psychological, and coaching services practice in 1997 that has grown to 100 employees. Our primary focus is on working with families and children. I work on the front lines and have observed increases in anxiety, panic attacks, depression, abuse of electronics and social media, and school problems. As disturbing as all of this sounds, I remain optimistic. As I have evolved, I have become increasingly aware of how important *face to face human interaction* is for mental fitness. I am reminded of Dan Beutner's revolutionary work as founder of *Blue Zones,* an organization that helps Americans live longer, healthier, happier lives. In his book, *The Blue Zones of Happiness—Lessons From the World's Happiest People,* Beutner shares extensive research on people living in the world's happiest places. He summarizes his greatest lessons learned in what he refers to as "The Happiness Power 9." Six of the nine elements of happiness involve making a connection with other human beings. In other words, we need each other! Discoveries in neuroscience corroborate this. We have learned that we are wired to each other neurologically, much like a bluetooth connection between electronic devices. The implication here is that we are able to use each other in relationships to heal. Our neural connections with our kids and their neural connections with others are what they need **most** to flourish in school; hence, their success requires more than just being smart. Herein lies the problem. Our children spend significantly more time with electronic devices than with us or others. Dr. Jean Twenge, whom I refer to several times in this book, estimates that our kids are three years behind socially and emotionally and are not prepared to move through adolescence to adulthood. Can you imagine your seventeen-year-old as a fourteen-year-old? Knowing this, it makes sense that our children are struggling in high school and on college campuses. Dr. Twenge refers to kids born after 1995 as the iGen or internet generation. These are children who have experienced their entire adolescence with the internet and cellphones. This exposure has not only led to deficits in critical social skills but also the poor physical health of our children as they are not spending enough time with each other or moving their bodies enough.

Our children need to be physically fit, psychologically sound, and socially connected to succeed in school. I take pains to prove this to you by presenting overwhelming evidence from research (in a relatable way) and personal experiences that have become the underpinnings of my eight-step parent coaching process. In this book, I work with you as I would if you were a coaching client. In chapter 1, I introduce the problems our iGen kids are facing, and in chapter 2, I write about some of my personal life experiences that have brought us together in this conversation. In chapter 3, I provide an outline of my mental fitness coaching framework, and in chapters 4 through 11, I engage you in the process. There are two core components: foundational skills and emotional intelligence skills. Foundational skills are the essential survival skills your child needs to learn before getting off to college. These skills include time management, sleep hygiene, nutrition, and physical activity. Although you may know a great deal about foundational skills, the bottom line is that our kids are struggling with them. Teens are the most sleep-deprived age group and get far less physical activity than required for optimal health. Time management was noted by my focus group participants as the number one challenge of the transition from high school to college. Also, we have long been aware of the obesity problem adults and children are struggling with in the US. My focus on these foundational skills is not as much about teaching as it is about helping you create sustainable structures with your child to help keep them on track. The heart of this book is in chapter 9, where I focus on emotional intelligence skills in great detail. Think of emotional intelligence as a mixture of social and emotional skills. Our kids need to be able to identify how they are feeling at any given moment and respond in a way that is beneficial to them. They need to be socially aware to learn how to interact effectively with others. Also, they need to develop empathy skills, not just for their own health, but for the health of the planet! I refer to Dr. Dan Goleman's visionary work on emotional intelligence. I make a strong case for emotional intelligence skills as more important than being "book smart" for your child to succeed in school and get into a good college.

When I finished my coffee, it was time to go to work. I walked into the lobby only to see a couple of moms sitting down next to their teen children wired into cell phones with heads down. I took a breath. I could feel the anxiety in the room and was moved to help. To me, there is nothing more sacred and powerful than the energy of a family. Typically, my first point of entry into a family system as a mental health professional, is through the "identified client." Take a guess as to who that usually is. Yeah, you got it… it's those darn teeny boppers! And Mama bear is the one who often brings them in. I can't tell you how much I have grown to admire and respect moms over the years in my work with families. Moms are so strong!

Don't get me wrong, dads are really important too! I am a dad myself with two daughters who have graduated from college within the past few years, and a son who is a sophomore. My wife and I have been truly blessed to be the *bow from which our children are sent forth*. My wish for you in reading this book is to be inspired and armed with the tools and strategies to send your children forth into college and a happy life beyond.

Chapter 1:
Time Is Running Out!

I received a phone call one day from a mom who was extremely frustrated with her sixteen-year-old son, Tommy. "I feel like time is running out! I don't think my son is going to be able to get into a good college!" She brought him into my office and sat in the lobby while I chatted with him. He was sitting slumped over in a chair with headphones on as I walked in. I asked him how he was doing, and he replied, "Really f...ing shitty!" His voice rang out so loud that it could be heard through the walls. I appreciated his authenticity and was able to join with him by thanking him for being so honest. He explained that his parents were always yelling at him and on his case: "I wish they would just get off my back." He spoke of how all they cared about was him looking good and getting good grades in school.

After listening to Tommy, I had his mom come into my office. She was wearing yoga pants and a blazer; a combination of athleticism and professionalism all in one. She seemed like a very strong person. I asked her to give me her take on what was going on with Tommy. As she started to speak, her face became red and tears welled up in her eyes, "I don't know what to do," she said. "I feel like my kid has gone crazy in the last year." She was frustrated by his lack of motivation and poor study habits. She went on to explain how he isolated himself in his room and was often impossible to have a conversation with. When he was in his room with the door shut, she was never sure if he was doing homework or using his cell phone. He slept late on weekends when he could be catching up with his schoolwork, and he often had his grades docked for handing assignments in late. "Right now, he's getting Cs and Ds in all of his classes," she said; "and I don't know how he thinks he's going to get into a good college!" She described his room as a disaster area and said she had been finding beer cans in his closet and "weird vaping" devices that she had never seen before. Overall, she reported feeling helpless and very worried about his future.

As I talked with Tommy's mom, she told me about a burning sensation she felt in her stomach every day. She'd been having problems sleeping and felt like she was getting a little depressed herself. Her relationship with her husband had been becoming more and more strained as they were unable to figure out how to help Tommy. I engaged her in a visualization by having her imagine her life a year from now as being so good that she rated it as a twelve on a scale of one to ten. I asked, "What would that look like?" She took a deep breath and said, "Tommy would be getting mostly As and maybe some Bs and getting into a good college." "And how would your life change?" I asked. She explained how relieved she would be to know that Tommy was going to get into a good college and would have a great future. "Tell me more," I said. "It would be a huge weight off of my shoulders not having to worry all of the time." She went on about being able to travel more with her husband as they reached their retirement years and hoped that she would not have to worry if Tommy was OK or not. "I think it would take the strain out of my marriage and hopefully create more intimacy in our relationship." More time for hobbies and self-care activities would be a dream compared to the stress she had been under for the past year with Tommy.

I worked with Tommy and his parents for a little over 6 months and, although it was challenging for all of us, the family made great strides. I worked hard to create a safe space for both Tommy and his parents to share their feelings and concerns. Despite all of their disagreements, the one goal they shared in common was that getting into a good college was important. Initially, Tommy felt like he was being punished and controlled by his parents. As he began to trust our process, he opened up about his intense fear of failure. He was overwhelmed by the size of the classes he attended in high school. It was often so loud in his classes that he couldn't concentrate and follow lesson plans. He was afraid to ask for help because he didn't want to look stupid. With tears in his eyes, he talked about being so far behind in school that he felt like there was nothing he could do to get back on track. His only forms of escape were video games, his cell phone, and social media. This was a defining moment for the family. Initially, Tommy's parents felt like he didn't care about anything and was being disrespectful and defiant. When they learned about Tommy's true feelings and fears, they became less reactive (i.e., they stopped yelling) and more empathetic and accepting. When Tommy became aware that they were truly an ally in his success, he bought into the plan. Over the next few months, Tommy and his parents were able to complete assignments together to improve communication with each other and work through conflicts and disagreements. Tommy accepted limits and structure around the behaviors, habits, and healthy routines necessary to succeed in school.

Sadly, the story of Tommy, his parents, and his bad grades is becoming a very common scenario in my practice, and people often avoid getting help. There can be multiple contributing factors to this problem. Although it is getting better, a social stigma continues to exist around asking for and receiving professional help. Disagreements can add fuel to the fire and keep parents from getting help. One parent often sees the other as coddling, while the other is seen as too strict. Sometimes, as parents, caught up in day-to-day activities, we simply don't see how much our kids are struggling. And our kids don't always have the tools to tell us what they are struggling with or what they need. Frequently, when we reach this stage with our children, we become overwhelmed. As parents trying to balance work, finances, household responsibilities, other children, aging parents, and one hundred other things, it is easy to become worn out and frustrated. Frustration can lead us to behave in ways that aren't always helpful for our children, such as yelling, engaging in power struggles, punishing, setting unrealistic limits, or inadvertently shaming our kids. When we cling to negative behavior patterns as a result of stress and frustration, we run the risk of intensifying problems and experiencing unintended consequences. Examples of escalated problems and unintended consequences for kids include high school dropouts, not getting accepted into colleges, mental health struggles, drug and alcohol abuse, loss of friends, loss of motivation, damaged self-esteem, negative peer groups, and legal problems. Examples of escalated problems and consequences for parents include high stress, depression and anxiety, work disturbances, marital conflict, and financial problems. This was the path Tommy's parents were on. Although they had good intentions for Tommy, they lost sight of how and where to direct their energy. Tommy's mom loved him so much and wanted nothing more than to see him succeed in school and in life. Unfortunately, it seemed like the harder she tried, the worse it got, and both she and her husband felt like they were nagging him all of the time. In Tommy's case, we were able to intervene before the family experienced serious consequences. I was touched by the courage Tommy's parents exhibited in stepping forward and facing their issues head on and praised them for their hard work.

If you have a child who has been struggling in school and doesn't seem like their old self, you are not alone. We are all well aware of the turbulence of being a teenager. That said, there are some unique circumstances in today's world covered in this book that have contributed to a record number of children unprepared to take on the rigors of the high school and college experience. We have all been hearing and reading about this new "internet generation" of kids born after 1995 who have grown up alongside the advent of the internet, cell phones, and other wireless devices. Dr. Jean Twenge, a researcher and psychology professor at San Diego State University, has studied generational differences for 25 years and coined the term "iGen," meaning "internet generation." iGen kids are the first to experience their entire adolescence on cell phones. Consequently, Dr. Twenge reports that kids have become more isolated from each other than previous generations, resulting in serious deficits in the social and emotional skills necessary to develop through adolescence and adulthood. These deficits are consistent with a historic increase in the mental health problems experienced by children and are presenting themselves in high schools and on college campuses with a spike in suicide and drop-out rates that run parallel to the technology boom. I have developed a mental fitness process to address these deficits and get your child on track to get into a good college. Let's begin by looking at a widely-accepted framework that illustrates how our children, under normal conditions, develop these very important social and emotional skills.

Abraham Maslow talks about the process of self-actualization as a theory of motivation. Self-actualization is something we all strive for as human beings, and as parents, we want very much for our children. To reach a level in life where we are doing what we were born to do, we have needs that have to be met along the way. Maslow presents it as a pyramid. We start at the bottom (1) and reach for the top (5):

1. **Physiological needs:** food, water, shelter, warmth, and sleep.

2. **Safety needs:** the need to feel secure, stable and unafraid.

3. **The need for love and belonging:** the need to belong socially by developing relationships with friends and family.

4. **Esteem needs:** need to feel both (a) self-esteem based on one's achievements and abilities and (b) recognition and respect from others.

5. **Self-actualization needs:** the need to pursue and fulfill one's unique potentials.

My mental fitness process shares similarities with Maslow's pyramid. We start at the bottom by making sure we have your child's basic needs in place by attending to foundational skills. Foundational skills correspond with Maslow's physiological and safety needs. They are the basic and very important skills your child needs to navigate through school life, such as managing time, getting good sleep, minding nutrition, and incorporating sufficient physical activity into daily routines.

A solid foundation lends itself to the development of confidence and healthy self-esteem. The second phase of my process focuses on the development of social and emotional skills, commonly called "emotional intelligence skills." These skills correspond with Maslow's love, belongingness, and esteem needs. Examples of emotional intelligence skills are self-aware-ness, self-management, social skills, and empathy. In moving through this process, you will understand how these skills are more important than being book smart and how they can set your child apart from others in succeeding in school, getting into a good college, and reaching the top of the pyramid.

Tommy's mom makes a good argument. Time is running out. The teenage years go by very quickly. It may not seem that way when we are in the trenches with our kids, feeling overwhelmed and tired. Don't worry. I am here to help you. I am not only here to help, but I am extremely excited to share this transformational process with you. In these next few years, you have an opportu-nity to rally and connect with your child like never before. If you were running a marathon and within a couple of miles of the finish line and I were your coach, I would be encouraging you and cheering you on. "Keep going! I know it's tiring! Don't give up. You're almost there! You've got this! It will be totally worth it! You'll be so happy that you stuck with it!" This is a defining moment in your marathon. I'm here with you. Let's do this!

Chapter 2:
Riding the Big Red with
A Sour Taste in My Mouth

I come from a very large Irish Catholic family. Growing up as a baby boomer, life was different back then. For example, we played outside with each other all the time, neighborhoods were like an extension of the family, and we were in each other's yards and houses on a daily basis. The families were also much larger, and kids were everywhere! Perhaps that's how I ended up in a profession as a psychologist and coach, that allows me to be around kids and families every day.

My mother was in her early twenties when she married my father, and by her early thirties, she had given birth to ten children. Imagine nine kids running around in a three-bedroom house, with two sets of triple-bunk beds, and always a crib or two with a baby. I had a twin brother who passed away a few days after we were born. We were both very small, and medical care for preemies wasn't nearly as advanced as it is today. I was a very active child, sometimes a bit too active. Unbeknownst to our family at the time, I later learned that I had Attention Deficit Hyperactivity Disorder (ADHD) and a non-verbal learning disability which manifests in significant visual-spatial deficits. Following an assessment I had as an adult, I was told, "David, an engineer you'll never be."

Although my family was low in monetary resources, we were rich in spirit. As much as we struggled financially, from a very young age, my parents instilled values of service in us. For that, I am eternally grateful! I would not trade my life experience for anything, for our experiences shape who we become and what we put out in the world. I will say though, that I have spent many years making mistakes and learning the hard way as I have strived to get to the top of my pyramid.

When I hit my teen years, I definitely had some struggles. I was disorganized, angry, impulsive, and living life with a chip on my shoulder. I also went through a phase of running away from home quite frequently. One night, after coming home drunk and angry, and threatening to run away again, my parents called the police. We got into a tussle. The police tried to be nice to me in front of my parents, but when we got to the squad car, they threw me in the back seat like a sack of potatoes. I don't really blame them because I was pretty incorrigible at the time. Ultimately, I ended up in a juvenile detention center, but the staff told me I was too nice to be there and they didn't know what to do with me. From there, I was moved to a shelter, followed by a treatment center for several months. Initially, I was defensive and resistant to receiving help and being honest with myself. As time went on, I began to develop trusting relationships with the adults in charge of my care. I responded to their positive feedback and the lessons they taught. I began to feel a more solid foundation under me. I was only fifteen years old at the time, and by the grace of God, I made it back home and graduated from high school.

I made my first attempt at college when I was nineteen years old. It was far more rigorous than high school and my foundation began to crumble. I got mostly F's my first semester and dropped out. I continued to enroll and drop out for the next several years, and my self-esteem was in the toilet! My soul sources of esteem and pleasure included running marathons and working out. Working as a waiter in a busy restaurant in Minneapolis, a few miles from the University of Minnesota, I met a local fitness celebrity who encouraged me to compete in a seven-week fitness contest at a popular night club. I gave it my all and I won. I was in orbit! Finally, I had achieved something to be proud of. My girlfriend at the time, who I was crazy in love with, shattered my world when I gave her the news. I thought she would be thrilled with my victory, however, to my chagrin, she said, "That's great, but if you don't get a college education, I don't think it's going to work out with us." I was crushed. I will never forget sitting on that city bus, the "Big Red," off to the University of Minnesota with a sour taste in my mouth, making yet another attempt at going to college. Following thirty-one years of marriage to her and having had my life transformed by the gift of education, I will always remember that conversation and that bus ride as a defining moment in my life.

I was almost thirty when I finally got my first college degree. I had to do remedial work in the General College at the University of Minnesota before getting into the College of Liberal Arts. For years, I was ashamed and thought I was stupid. I used to avoid my friends, who had since graduated and entered the workforce as young professionals. One day, after coming home from school, feeling exhausted and disheveled, I had a spiritual moment. As I laid down on my bed, I was sweating, my heart was pounding, my stomach was in knots, and my brain was racing. I was thinking the same old negative thoughts about failure. But this time, in my exhaustion, I surrendered. I told God I didn't know what to do and

I wanted to give up. Immediately, I began to feel a warmth spread throughout my body. I was enveloped by a sense of calm. The only way I can describe it is that I felt God's presence telling me that everything was going to be OK. I took solace in the fact that I was doing absolutely everything I could do to make it. From that moment on, I learned to love myself no matter what. I stopped avoiding people, and when they asked what I was doing, I was one hundred percent honest with them: "I'm working in a restaurant and going to school." I can't tell you how freeing it was for me to be brutally honest with myself and others around me. Everything in life got easier after that. After I became licensed as a psychologist and certified as a coach, I made it my personal life's mission to help others reach the top of their pyramid.

I hope you don't think I'm sharing my story to convey that you have to come from an economically-challenged background to experience adversity and struggle in school and life. Adversity does not discriminate. I see people from every background imaginable in my practice who struggle: under-resourced kids, well-resourced kids, kids from all races, kids who have experienced trauma, and kids with mental health problems. All kids, regardless of where they come from or what their situation is, need to be physically healthy, psychologically sound, and socially connected to reach the top of their pyramid. In my case, our family was poor in terms of monetary resources and I had undiagnosed ADHD and a learning disability. In Tommy's case, his family had lots of resources but were unaware of how isolated and overwhelmed he was. The bottom line is that we were both struggling mightily to move up on our pyramids. We all have our unique struggles, regardless of our background. In this book, and in this process we are going through together, I want to help you reflect on how you are doing, how your child is doing, and what some of the unique struggles teens and young adults are facing in today's world that impact their ability to succeed in school. I have learned, personally and professionally, that succeeding in school is much more than being book smart. And the good news is that there is much we can do for our kids that we sometimes lose sight of in our busy lives that will help them achieve good grades and get into good colleges.

The fact that you are reading this book tells me that you love your child and are invested in their mental fitness and success in school and in life. I offer this coaching process for all parents and teens. We have to face the truth and acknowledge that our internet generation kids are experiencing stressors that have compromised their ability to succeed in school and other aspects of life. And we have to face the truth that as adults and parents, we have been affected by technology in much the same way. I have three children who have moved through adolescence into young adulthood. As I raised them, I was caught off guard by the negative impact that the internet, cell phones, and other forms of wireless technology can have. We can be the most well-meaning, knowledgeable parents in the world and still disconnect with our kids when we are busy.

My life's work has been about empowering and motivating people to be healthy and succeed in all aspects of life. Yet, with all of this knowledge and personal experience, I hire therapists, coaches, and personal trainers when I need help. For me, it's about creating a structure and keeping my awareness up on a daily basis until I get where I want to be. One of the most gratifying and special experiences of my life was receiving some therapy as I was in the throes of a PhD program. I was so intensely busy and disconnected that I seriously strained my relationship with my oldest daughter who was about to head off to college. I rolled up my sleeves and worked hard on myself and my relationship with my daughter for a period of 6 months. It changed my life and created an incredible bond that we now share as adults. If you jump in and commit to this experience, you will not only be helping your child succeed in school and college but you will also create a special bond as they leave the nest and move into adulthood.

Chapter 3:
Mental Fitness Is Key

A popular framework in the field of counseling and psychology used to assess mental fitness is a "bio/psycho/social" framework. This basically means that mentally fit kids are physically healthy, mentally strong, have good friends, and get along well with others. Your child needs to be mentally fit to succeed in school. A mental fitness approach focuses more on assessing and building on your child's strengths as opposed to spending more time on shortcomings.

In this book, two of the core components of the mental fitness process outlined for you and your child are foundational and emotional intelligence skills. Foundational skills are the basic survival skills your child needs to navigate through high school and college; these include time management, nutrition, sleep hygiene, and physical activity. I introduced these skills briefly in chapter 1. These skills are at the bottom of the pyramid, hence, they are foundational skills. I will go into more detail on how to instill these skills in your child in chapter 8. Emotional intelligence skills have to do with how well your child is functioning socially and emotionally. These are the higher-level skills illustrated on the pyramid. I will discuss these at length in chapter 9. Teens need to be able to manage emotions to cope with stress and to be socially aware to get along with others. These are critical skills that have fallen to the wayside with the advent of the internet, cell phones, and other forms of wireless technology, and have resulted in major problems in high schools and on college campuses. Dr. Jean Twenge, in her book, *iGen: Why Today's Super-Connected Kids Are Growing Up Less Rebellious, More Tolerant, Less Happy – And Completely Unprepared for Adulthood*, notes that today's teens are experiencing a three-year delay in developing the critical social and emotional skills required to progress through adolescence into adulthood.

Why Focus on Mental Fitness?

According to Centers for Disease Control (CDC), "today's college students are suffering from an epidemic of mental illnesses. Evidence reveals that 15 to 24-year-olds are experiencing a greater level of stress and psychopathology than at any other time in history." The CDC then goes on to state that, "suicide is the third leading cause of death behind accidents and homicide of people aged 15 to 24." Furthermore, "One in four students has a diagnosable mental illness, 40 percent do not seek out help, and 50 percent have become so anxious that it has caused serious struggles in school within the past year." Currently, colleges and universities are reporting a record number of students coming in unprepared and dropping out. They are overwhelmed by the prevalence of mental health struggles on campuses and report not being able to meet the needs of kids who are seeking out mental health support.

I know. It's alarming. Please... don't shoot the messenger. This is a reality that we all have to face as parents, educators, coaches, mentors, and mental health professionals. In Chapter 6, I will go into more detail about the current-day stressors our teens and young adults are facing that have contributed to this crisis.

The *best* way to ensure your child will get good grades and excel in high school is to parent for mental fitness. Mentally-fit kids have higher grade point averages and get into better colleges. Not only that, but they also present themselves better in job interviews and compete more effectively in the workplace following college graduation. The mental fitness process offered to you in this book will help your child get a solid foundation under them and up to speed socially and emotionally for success in school. As you come along with me on this ride, you will learn to:

- Help your iGen child overcome the barriers to achieving good grades.

- Implement parenting strategies that will motivate your child to work hard at getting good grades.

- Work through conflict with your child so that they can stay on track with school work.

- Develop an easy to follow organizational plan to help your child get good grades.

- Help your child get accepted into a good college.

There is more than one way to use this book. The first three steps are about reflecting on the big picture before you move into action with your child. I offer journaling exercises for most chapters. I highly recommend you do them and save them for review as you move through the steps. Journaling will help you identify issues and gain clarity on your thoughts and feelings. It will also assist you in measuring your progress along the way. Steps four through eight are a collaboration between you and your child. The focus is on promoting mental fitness and your child's success in school. My suggestion for you, as a parent coaching your child through this process, is to set some goals that you can participate in with them. This may help you engage your child. We can all benefit from paying better attention to foundational skills, and this could be a point of entry for you. For example, you could work on getting more exercise and better nutrition and share your progress together weekly. You can either move through this process sequentially, or pick out reference points that are a fit for what is needed.

Chapter 4:
Step 1—What's Happening
with Your Child?

When your child is struggling in school and you feel like you can't help them, it's perfectly normal to get in overwhelm mode. The first step in my mental fitness process is to have you reflect on what you see happening with your child and be clear about what you want for them. I chose to open this chapter with a complex client story that covers several problems pertinent to our children. As you read the case study below, as well as the subsequent problem discussions, think about your child. What parts of the story resonate with you? What are your concerns for your child? What are your hopes and dreams?

Case Study: Jack

I received a referral from a social worker at a local high school one day following a fight that occurred in the locker room after a hockey practice. Jack came in with his mom. It was clear he did not want to have anything to do with seeing a counselor. Initially, he refused to participate and became very angry, yelling and swearing loudly in the lobby. I let him sit down and cool off while I spoke with his mother. Her shoulders shook as she sobbed in my office. I felt really bad for her. "Jack got into a fight at school. He got suspended and kicked off of the hockey team." Jack was a very talented hockey player and was being scouted by several Division One hockey programs. "He hasn't been the same since the divorce!" Mom explained that her ex-husband had a drinking problem and had been cheating on her for several years. After a heated argument in which he threw her against the wall in a drunken rage, she called it quits.

Jack's life had spiraled downward within the past year. "He has a temper just like his father's." Apparently, this hadn't been the first fight he had been in since the divorce. His most recent fight was precipitated by a photograph one of his teammates took from a Snapchat post at a drinking party. In the picture, Jack had no clothes on, and it was shared globally around school. Kids call these "noods." Texting nude pictures is a growing and concerning trend among both male and female teens in middle and high schools. "It is like he just went on strike after the divorce," his mom explained. Jack was flunking most of his classes and was drinking alcohol on a regular basis. Mom was really worried about his safety. She reported that when he gets drunk, he says things that make her think he is going to hurt himself or commit suicide. Mom continued to sob in my office. "I feel like I've lost my son. I feel like he's not the same person!" I asked her what her hopes and dreams were for Jack. She explained that it would mean the world for her to see him get into a good college. Jack's scholarship was a great way to make it happen. "I want him to be a lifelong learner and I hope he finds someone to love and has a good marriage." She talked about how all of his hockey coaches throughout the years would always tell her how driven he is, and what a great leader he was on the ice. "If he could just take that out into the world, I would be so happy!"

I worked for some time with Jack's mother to help her try to get him back on track. We had some unraveling to do.

Problem Discussion #1: Divorce

There's really no set way that kids react when their parents get divorced. Some act out, some withdraw, and some don't seem to be affected very much. Jack acted out very angrily. When we peeled back the layers of the onion, we discovered he was very hurt and grieving. His mom likened his behavior to "going on strike." Nothing mattered anymore, including school. This is not an uncommon reaction for kids within the first 6 months to a year following a divorce. And sometimes, as a parent, it's like you have to be bilingual. Kids may say one thing and mean another. Mom's reaction to Jack's anger initially wasn't working because she couldn't understand him and had a hard time not taking his behavior personally. I coached her to try to respond to his anger as if he were telling her he was hurt and sad, and to check whether his reaction was different. Eventually, I was able to get both of Jack's parents into my office, and although there was tension, they were able to come together to improve the way they were co-parenting. We get emotional as parents and sometimes have a hard time keeping our kids out of the middle of our disputes. This had been a great source of stress for Jack. His parents both very much wanted him to get back on track and became better at maintaining healthy boundaries.

Problem Discussion #2: Suicidal Talk

Teen suicide has spiked dramatically within the past decade. And according to Centers for Disease Control (CDC), mental health problems in teens and young adults has reached epidemic levels. I will talk more about this in Chapter 6. If your child mentions or alludes to suicide, take it seriously and have a chat with them. As mental health professionals, we look at suicidal talk as existing on a continuum from "suicidal ideation" (i.e., having thoughts about suicide) to "intent" (i.e., having a plan). There is a big difference between these two. If you see some red flags, be direct: "Jack, I'm concerned... have you been thinking about suicide?" Often kids say they feel like they want to be dead or "if I died, I wouldn't care." This is an example of ideation. The next step for you as a parent is to ask them if they have thought about a way to do it; a plan. If they verbalize a plan, keep chatting to determine if they have a means to follow through with their plan. If they have a plan and have a means to follow through, seek out help immediately. Options range from calling a crisis line, to taking your child to the nearest emergency room, or dialing 911, depending on the severity of your situation. In Jack's case, he had ideation, but no plan. I recommended mom check in with him daily to see how he was feeling. I checked in with Jack and his mom weekly in our sessions until he no longer reported ideation.

Problem Discussion #3: Substance Use

Jack's mom asked me, "Do you think my son is an alcoholic?" Upon hearing this, I spoke with her about the difference between abuse and dependency. A lot of teens binge drink and get intoxicated. When substance use becomes so serious and prevalent that it impairs someone's ability to function in major life areas, such as work, school, relationships, or maintaining health, we start looking at it as dependency. Dealing with substance use with teens is tricky. If they are in danger with substance use, and self-destructive, chemical dependency treatment is a good idea for safety reasons and to provide education. The reality is that most teens who go through chemical dependency treatment do not remain abstinent for the rest of their lives. Diversion is another way to look at coping with addictive behaviors in kids. The more socially-engaged kids are in school, sports, hobbies, and other things they like to do, the easier it is to stay away from harmful substances. It is no fun to have something you like taken away, especially when you are struggling emotionally and if it makes you feel better. If something is added that is more important or exciting, it can naturally push the substance away without feeling like something is being taken from you. Jack's alcohol use was risky and dangerous. And the fact that his father struggled with alcohol was an additional risk factor. Substance use and mental health struggles can pass through generations. I coached Jack's mom to think about working with him around chemical use as an ongoing process where she would assist him in learning from consequences and developing strategies to be safe. I continued to assess Jack's chemical use and related consequences as our work progressed. He was able to learn from his mistakes and utilize diversionary activities to curb his substance use. I coached his parents to facilitate a meeting between Jack and his hockey coach. Eventually, Jack got back on the hockey team and committed himself to abstinence from alcohol and drugs during the season.

Problem Discussion #4: Mental Health

In addition to wondering if he was an alcoholic or not, Jack's mom wanted to know if he had depression. It is normal for your child to experience depression or anxiety in their teen years. As in our discussion about chemical use, if it gets to a point where it is seriously jeopardizing your child's ability to function in school, in a job, in relationships, or causes serious physical health threats, getting professional help is a good idea. I assessed Jack for depression and anxiety. While he was experiencing symptoms of both, he didn't fit the full criteria for either diagnosis. Instead, Jack's condition more accurately fit the diagnostic criteria for adjustment disorder with mixed disturbance of emotions and conduct. In other words, Jack was reacting to situational stressors such as the divorce of his parents and the pressures of high school. My prescription for Jack was to participate in individual and family therapy without medication. Had Jack's symptoms persisted or worsened within the course of therapy, I would have referred him for a medication assessment.

Summary

Were you able to identify with any parts of this story? Although Jack's case was extreme and covered many important problem areas experienced by teens, it was by no means a comprehensive study. Your child may have some struggles not mentioned in Jack's case. If you want to help your child overcome their struggles and succeed in school, you will need to learn about sources of stress. In order to learn about the sources of stress your teen is experiencing and how they are coping, it is very important to have honest and open conversations with them.

Assignment

Below is a list of common triggers of teen stress taken from an article by Dr. Kathleen Smith. Use this list as an assessment tool by having a discussion with your child about each of these stressors. Have your child rate each area on a scale of 0 to 10, where 0 is no stress at all and 10 is the highest possible stress they could experience. List the numbers in your journal that most closely reflect your child's stress rating under each topic. You and your child can take this assessment again at the end of this process to measure your progress.

- **Academic Stress**

From grades to test scores to applying to college, teens experience high levels of school-related stress. Many teens worry about meeting academic demands, pleasing teachers and parents, and keeping up with their classmates. Poor time management skills can also play into academic stress.

- **Social Stress**

Teens place a high value on their social lives and spend the majority of their waking hours among their peers. Finding and keeping their tribes can be stressful. Bullying and subtle instances of relational aggression are clear sources of stress. Learning to manage conflict and work through romantic relationships are also significant sources of stress on developing teens. Peer pressure is an additional stress during the teen years. In an effort to establish and maintain friendships, teens can engage in risk taking behavior to fit in.

- **Family Problems**

Unrealistic expectations, marital problems, strained sibling relationships (including sibling bullying), illness in the family, and financial stress on the family can all trigger a spike in teen stress.

- **World Events**

   School shootings, acts of terrorism, and natural disasters worry parents, but they also trigger stress for teens. Teens are often privy to the 24-hour news cycle, and hearing bits and pieces of scary news, both domestic and abroad, can leave teens wondering about their safety and the safety of their loved ones.

- **Traumatic Events**

   Death of a family member or friend, accidents, sickness, or enduring emotional or physical abuse can have a lasting impact on teen stress levels. It's also important to note that teen dating violence affects approximately 10% of teens.

- **Significant Life Changes**

   Like adults, teens experience stress due to significant life changes. Moving, starting at a new school, and changes in the makeup of the family (including divorce and blended families) can trigger stress for teens. Not knowing how to cope with big changes is overwhelming and can be confusing for your child.

   Chapter 4 Journal Exercise: When you finish this assessment, continue writing in your journal on the following: What are your concerns for your child? What are your hopes and dreams?

Chapter 5:
Step 2—What's Happening in Your World?

What's Your Style?

Based on our childhood experiences, we develop parenting styles. Much has been written in research about parenting styles and many categories have been designated. In an effort to keep things simple, I am going to share three styles from developmental psychologist Dr. Diana Baumrind. These are the most common ones I run into in my practice. As you learn about them, think about how they relate to how you were parented, and the impact they have on your current parenting style. What I don't want you to do is cement yourself into any one of these categories. Remember, we are not perfect. Sometimes we are on a roll as parents, doing a good job, and sometimes we struggle and make mistakes. This is about becoming more self-aware so we can be more effective in helping our kids through school.

- *Authoritarian/strict and controlling:* This style has been linked to the most unfortunate consequences for healthy child development. It is characterized by parents having a high need for behavioral control and a strict family hierarchy. Parents implement strict rules and leave no room for discussion with their kids. Parents encourage the suppression of emotions, while they can also become aggressive and angry with their kids. Rules are typically enforced via threats and with punishment. Kids of authoritarian parents quickly learn to adjust to the parent's expectations. In other words, they are well-behaved out of fear: "If I don't behave, I will be punished!" They tend to willingly obey authorities. They have internalized and accepted the prevailing norm and value system, which means they do relatively well in school and do not engage in deviant behavior such as criminal acts or experimental drug or alcohol use. They are not used to making independent choices or taking full responsibility for themselves. They do not experiment much with new ways of doing things or alternative ways of thinking. According to research, kids of authoritarian parents are not as socially skilled as kids from authoritative and permissive families. They find it difficult to handle frustration: girls tend to give up in the face of challenges and boys tend to react with aggressiveness. They are also more prone to suffering from low self-esteem, anxiety, and depression.

- **Permissive:** Permissive parents are at the other end of the spectrum. They believe in the autonomy of the individual. To them, they see the world as a free place filled with opportunities just waiting to be seized. Permissive parents believe in responding to their children's desires in an accepting and feeling manner. Traditional child discipline and rigid rules of conduct are seen as restrictive of a child's natural development and free, independent thinking. Children are perceived as equals and are included in decision-making processes and are encouraged to communicate and discuss, rather than just obey. Permissive parents dislike and tend to avoid confrontations and the overt use of power to shape and regulate their child's behavior. Kids who have a lack of limits, an absence of authority figures, and no consistent routines or predictability, may experience a sense of insecurity: "How far can I go and what can I count on?" In response to a parent who avoids conflict, the child may become bossy or dominating as he or she tries to search for limits where there are none. Children of permissive parents are found to be more impulsive and involved in problematic behavior, such as drug and alcohol use, and do less well in school than kids from authoritative and authoritarian parents. As these kids are brought up in the belief that they are adult equals, they are well equipped in dialogue, have high social skills and high self-esteem and low levels of depression.

- *Authoritative:* Most parenting experts agree that this is the most effective style. Just like the authoritarian parents, the authoritative parent's control is firm and the standards of behavior are high. The difference is that authoritative parents are not keeping their children down or restricting them as a sort of preventative measure for bad behavior. The authoritative parents strive towards letting their children live out their potentials but within an overall controlled framework: "You can go as far as this point, but exceeding this boundary will not be tolerated." In this way, the authoritative parents recognize that a child needs to have a degree of say but will always make sure to have the final word. They strive to balance a child's need for autonomy and their own need for discipline and control. Authoritative parents use praise and positive attention as a way to make their child want to behave well: "If I behave and do well, I will get positive attention." Authoritative parents make an effort to understand their child and teach them how to understand their own feelings. They encourage problem solving and independence. Because of the use of positive reinforcement (praise) along with logical and fair rules done in a warm, caring manner, the child has learned that behaving and following rules feels good and gets them positive attention. Their ability to decode, and subsequently, live up to their parent's rules and expectations, provides them with well-developed social skills and emotional regulation. According to research, kids of authoritative parents do well in school, are self-confident, and goal-oriented.

What's Your Story?

We all grow up with a unique set of circumstances that become our story, and our story has an impact on how we parent our children. Being an effective parent isn't as much about whether you had a good or bad childhood. It's more about reflecting and looking back and connecting the dots. It's about recognizing how your experience as a child gets replayed in your mind as you are engaging with your teen. You might think, "Oh. OK. This is the same thing I experienced when I was that age. That's why I get triggered when my daughter talks back," or "Oh, I see, my mom used to get terrified when I didn't come home on time and would yell and scream at me. That's why I get so scared when my child doesn't come home on time." When we are able to understand how we get from point A to point B (connecting the dots), we can step back and check ourselves without feeling like we are failures as parents. When we get frustrated and yell at our kids, most of the time it's about us, not them. As a parent, I try not to yell at my kids and have been mostly successful, but have not always been perfect. Have you ever yelled at your child and all of a sudden, your mom or dad pops into your head? You think to yourself, "I can't believe it. I'm doing exactly what I said I would never do." The point I am trying to make here is, if you aren't aware of where you have been, then you are more likely to be reactive versus proactive.

Richard's Story

This is a story with an unhappy ending. Richard was referred to me for parent coaching by a friend of his with whom I had worked successfully some years back. Richard was in his mid-forties and the father of two adolescent boys. Prior to coming to see me, Richard had been experiencing a great deal of conflict with his younger son. I engaged Richard in several discussions exploring his family of origin and how he was parented as a child. Richard described his parents as "old school." His mother worked part-time at the neighborhood grocery store, but mostly stayed home to take care of the family. His father was a hard-working man who owned a small construction company and drank heavily on the weekends. Richard spoke lovingly of his parents, but it was clear that he was raised in an authoritarian environment where physical punishment was administered frequently. At one point in our discussions, Richard said of his father, "Man, he could hit hard and yell like nobody's business!" Richard described his mother as sweet and loving. He would go to her for comfort after receiving physical punishment from his dad. When his father wasn't around, Richard's mom treated him like an adult and allowed him to pretty much do whatever he wanted.

As our work progressed, Richard shared stories about his relationship with his children as they grew from infancy to adolescence. As little kids, if they misbehaved, he would give them a swat on their behind, a slap on the hand, or yell at them sternly. He felt like he was doing the right thing at the time because they would comply. When they reached adolescence, the power struggles escalated and his attempts at controlling his children's behavior became more severe. Yelling turned into screaming and swats turned into more physical forms of punishment. His older child would usually get in line, but his younger child began to rebel. The more defiant and oppositional his son was, the more extreme Richard's disciplinary tactics became. At his core, Richard loved his children deeply and would feel remorseful after punishing them harshly. In an attempt to make it up to them, he would give them gifts, be permissive, and overlook many of the household rules that he and his wife had agreed upon.

In my efforts to get Richard to connect the dots, I had him examine his parenting methods and compare them to how he was raised. His harsh disciplinary practices mirrored his father's style, while his attempts to make up for it reflected his mother's style. This was very confusing not only for his son, but for the rest of the family. Although Richard was able to talk about how his father had strict control of his family and how he was mistreated, he was unable to see how he had recreated the same dynamic in his family and unwilling to make the necessary changes. Unfortunately, his youngest son, who was struggling in school and in the community, eventually left home. They continue to be estranged from one another.

My Story

I went through a turbulent period of time with my son as he was entering early adolescence. He was doing what teens do—testing limits and taking some risks—but nothing really out of the norm for teen behavior. We had a period of time where I would get mad and yell at him. As a mental health professional and a coach, a little voice in my head was telling me that yelling was not helpful. I struggled for a few months to keep my composure with him. We finally had a chat one day. He told me that he felt demoralized when I yelled at him. Yelling made him want to rebel rather than comply. Intuitively, I knew this to be true, yet it was difficult for me to check myself in the heat of the moment. When I reflected back on my experiences growing up, it became clear to me that, like Richard's father, my father leaned more towards the authoritarian style. There were so many of us to take care of and he felt like he needed to be strict to keep us safe and under control. I was a very active child (remember, undiagnosed ADHD) and some of my impulsive behaviors got me into trouble. Looking back at it, I probably scared my dad half to death! While he never used physical punishment, I was yelled at and frequently grounded for long periods of time.

In my own experience of connecting the dots, I realized that I was triggered by my son's entry into adolescence. Ages fourteen and fifteen were the rockiest period in my teen years, and my son's behavior was really pushing my buttons. My yelling was more about me than his behavior. I was unconsciously recreating my family dynamic. After some practice and deep breathing, I began to yell less. It greatly improved our communication.

As parents, we don't need to condemn ourselves for making mistakes and yelling at our children. Most of us have been there. What we need to realize is that we don't have to be right all of the time with our kids. We can apologize and mend fences. And while yelling may stop a behavior in the moment, it doesn't teach our kids the behaviors we are looking for. It is impossible to communicate and express love through harsh discipline. Our children are more willing to listen to us and accept limits if they feel loved and understood.

Chapter 5 Journal Exercise: How has your childhood experience benefited your parenting style? Which of your childhood experiences do you need to be aware of that may result in making mistakes? What example do you want to set for your kids? What values do you want to pass on to them?

Chapter 6:
Step 3—Understanding Your iGen's Unique World

According to the Center for Generational Kinetics, "a generation is a group of people *born* around the same time and *raised* around the same place. People in this "birth cohort" exhibit similar characteristics, preferences, and values over their lifetimes." For example, I am a Baby Boomer. We are individuals who were born between 1946 and 1964, who grew up with the Beatles, the Vietnam war, Woodstock, and the Apollo moon landings. We were profoundly impacted by television. The generation following me is Generation X, born between 1961 and 1980. Generation X witnessed the end of the cold war, the fall of the Berlin Wall, Live Aid, and the personal computer. Next up is Generation Y, more commonly referred to as Millennials. These folks were born between 1981 and 1995. Their formative experiences were the 9/11 terroristic attacks, the Sony PlayStation, social media, and reality TV.

The focus of this chapter is on the current generation and its unique influences and challenges. Dr. Jean Twenge, a professor of psychology at San Diego State University, coined the term "iGen," referring to kids born after 1995 who have grown up with cell phones and can't remember a time without access to the internet. Common characteristics of iGeners are:

- Much more tolerant of others (e.g., different cultures, sexual orientations, and races).

- Much more cautious, less risk taking.
- Less drinking and drug taking in high school.
- Less likely to go to church.
- More likely to think for themselves and not believe authority figures in church or government.
- Delaying having serious romantic relationships.
- Less teen pregnancy.
- Fewer run-aways.
- Delaying driving, and fewer teen driving accidents.
- Less time spent in shopping malls.
- Less likely to go out to see a movie.
- More likely to use Instagram than Facebook.
- Less "in person" and "face to face" contact with others due to more time connecting via smartphones.
- Heavy use of gaming.
- Less reading of books and newspapers.
- Grew up more supervised and more protected than prior generations.
- Less experience with teen jobs and earning money in high school.
- May stay up until 2 AM using their smartphone and social media.

Challenge Discussion #1: Cell phones and social media

In her book, Dr. Twenge identifies eleven major trends with our iGen kids. One of the most alarming trends she talks about that has negatively impacted school performance in our children is a dramatic decline in social and emotional skills. Social and emotional skills are more important than being book smart for your child to succeed, not only in school but also in the workplace after they get out of college. Through her research, Dr. Twenge has estimated that our kids are three years behind both socially and emotionally. Imagine your fifteen-year-old on a college campus! There is strong evidence that cell phones and other forms of wireless technology are the culprits. Kids are spending more time with their cell phones than with each other. Take a look at these trends:

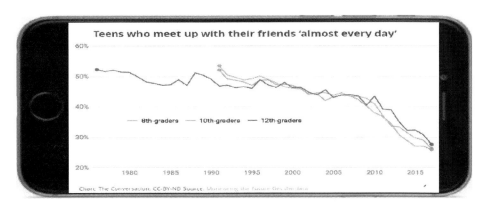

Teens who meet up with their friends 'almost every day'

The numbers on the left of this diagram represent the percentages of teens who spend time with their friends almost every day. The numbers on the bottom represent the years beginning from 1980 to 2015. Since the mid-1990s, there has been a dramatic decrease in the percentages of kids who spend time with each other almost every day. In the early to mid-1990s, approximately 54% of teens met up with their friends regularly. By 2015, the percentage of teens meeting regularly dropped by nearly 30%. And look at the reverse trend below.

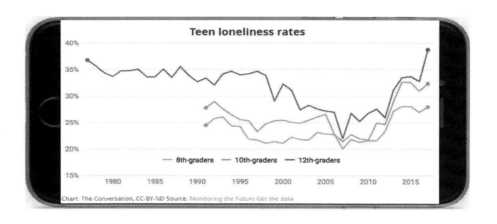

Teen loneliness rates have skyrocketed! Take note of the spike from 2010 to 2015. According to the Pew Research Center, smartphone ownership crossed the 50 percent threshold in late 2012, right when teen depression and suicide began to rise. By 2015, 73 percent of teens had access to smartphones. And as teen loneliness has gone up, so has the prevalence of mental health disorders. According to Dr. Keith Anderson, President of the American College Health Association Survey, one in three college freshmen reported having suffered from mental health disorders prior to coming to college.

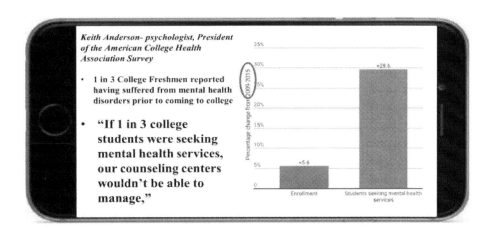

From 2009 to 2015, students seeking mental health services in colleges went up 29.6 percent. Colleges are not even close to being able to handle this demand. There appears to be a correlation between the increase in mental health issues and suicide rates, as illustrated by the diagram below.

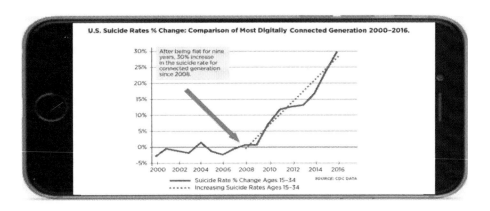

As you can see, suicide rates were relatively flat from 1999 to 2008. From 2009 to 2016, the suicide rate for teens and young adults went up by 30 percent, which is almost 100 percent consistent with the ratio of kids seeking out mental health services in colleges.

I am not a research scientist. My intent in giving you this information is not to tell you that cell phones and wireless technology have caused this spike in mental health struggles, school problems, and suicides. To come to such a conclusion, you have to conduct scientific studies and have them evaluated by the research community. That said, these are trends we cannot ignore. When I look at the data, I see an alarming series of trends that appear to be the formula for a perfect storm:

- Increased screen time leads to less face-to-face contact.
- Less face-to-face contact leads to increased loneliness.
- Increased loneliness leads to a decrease in social and emotional skills.
- Decreases in social and emotional skills lead to increases in mental health disorders and problems in high schools and on college campuses.
- Increases in mental health disorders leads to an increase in suicide rates.

In 1995, at the onset of the iGeneration, Dr. Dan Goleman, a modern-day guru on the subject of social and emotional skills, wrote the book: *Emotional Intelligence – Why It Can Matter More Than IQ*. Here is a quote from his book: "Will these tech-savvy children become adults who are as comfortable with other people as they are with their computers? I suspected that a childhood relating to the virtual world, would deskill our young people when it comes to relating to people." It appears as if his suspicions were right on the money!

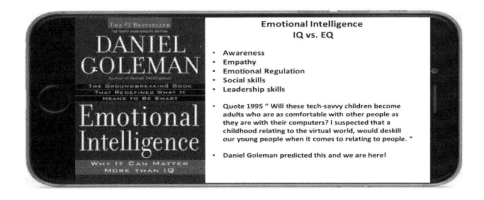

This is a topic that is being heavily researched, and we will be getting more information moving forward. Dr. Twenge, in her research, has noted that problems begin to occur when screen time exceeds over two hours per day. How much screen time is your child engaging in each day? How much screen time are you engaging in each day?

Challenge Discussion #2: Teen Brain

As you are coaching your child to become more mentally fit and succeed in school, it is important to have some basic information about brain biology. We now are aware that the brain doesn't fully develop until about age twenty-five. Below is a visual aid to look at to help you understand how your child's brain develops.

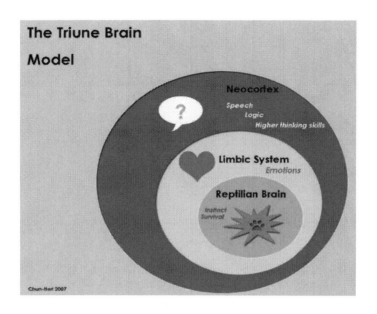

The Triune Brain Model

Neocortex
Speech
Logic
Higher thinking skills

Limbic System
Emotions

Reptilian Brain
Instinct
Survival

Chun-Itori 2007

Much like our earlier discussion of Maslow's pyramid, the brain develops from the bottom up. The bottom or lower brain has been referred to by researchers as the reptilian brain. This is because reptiles were among the first life forms on the planet. Think about a lizard sitting on a rock sunning itself. Not the cute Geico lizard that you see in commercials who has been infused with human qualities, but an actual lizard. It simply sits in the sun. It's not concerned about what it is going to wear to school tomorrow. It doesn't feel sad because its best friend ghosted her on Instagram. It doesn't feel love or loyalty to its family. Its only concern is survival: eating, breathing, keeping warm and reproducing. As infants, this is the primary part of the brain we function from.

As our children mature into the pre-teen and teen years, brain development occurs in the limbic system. The "limbic system" is the emotional part of the brain. This is the part of the brain that feels emotions, empathy, the need for social connection, and a sense of values. This is also the part of the brain where kids can get stuck. It's like a Neanderthal, with very raw emotions. And while they have a need for social affiliation, they are not skilled enough to express emotions appropriately. Think of an adolescent boy attempting to show an adolescent girl that he likes her by patting her on the back roughly, like he would do with one of his buddies, or bringing her a dead frog as a gift.

The neocortex, the outer part of the brain, is the most sophisticated and highly developed part of the brain. This is the part of the brain that utilizes logic, searches for meaning, and makes rational decisions. This is where we want to be as we mature as adults.

Neuropsychiatrist Dr. Dan Siegal refers to the adolescent brain as a "brain under construction." Development starts from the base of the brain, moving up towards the front from lower to higher-level functions. The end goal is the development of an "integrated brain." Emotions are mediated by rational thought for the sake of our children's ability to control impulses and make sound decisions. Teens with lesser developed thinking and planning parts of their brains have a much quicker route to their emotional center, resulting in what has been referred to by researchers and clinicians as "limbic lava." Teenagers are predisposed to volcanic eruptions of raw emotion that can get quite hot. It is the job of the higher-order thinking and planning part of the brain (neocortex) to cool the limbic lava. When our children are unable to cope with raw emotions and think rationally, they need guidance and support to make good decisions.

I vividly remember the day my 16-year-old daughter came home from her driver's license test. She had not only just passed, but had done it on her first attempt. She was ecstatic! I stopped her in mid-sprint as she grabbed my car keys from the kitchen table. We were both simultaneously incensed. I, by her new found sense of entitlement over driving, and she, for being questioned. After all, she had just passed her test. What could possibly go wrong now? Sparks were flying to say the least! Brain-based researchers would agree that, in that moment, my daughter and I were having a failure to communicate from a biological perspective. Although adolescent brain-based research is in its infancy, it is well established that the emotional center of the brain in the limbic system matures earlier than the higher-order thinking and planning part of the brain (neocortex). Activated limbic lava made it very difficult for my daughter to focus and answer the "who, what, when, where, and why" of my questions. "How can you not let me go? I just passed my test! Please, just let me go!" I assisted her by taking a breath, slowing myself down, and providing an explanation for my questions. When she became convinced that it was about her safety, she participated with me in making a plan.

Knowledge of limbic lava does not give us a pass to ignore our teen's eruptions, nor for them to erupt whenever they want. If we view these eruptions as events that must be corrected immediately, however, we could inadvertently be setting ourselves and our children up for failure. If we view our teenager's development not as an event but an ongoing process, we will have better success. An adolescent's path to a fully developed thinking and planning part of the brain can take 10-15 years, and can extend into the mid-twenties.

Challenge Discussion # 3: Bullying

In an article from *Psychology Today*, bullying is described as "a distinctive pattern of harming and humiliating others; specifically, those who are in some way smaller, weaker, younger, or in any way more vulnerable than the bully. Bullying is not garden-variety aggression; it is a deliberate and repeated attempt to cause harm to others of lesser power. It's a very durable behavioral style, largely because bullies get what they want, at least at first. Bullies are made, not born, and it happens at an early age, if normal aggression of 2-year-olds isn't handled with consistency. Between 1 in 4 and 1 in 3 students in the United States reports being bullied at school, according to the National Center for Education Statistics and Bureau of Justice Statistics. In grades 6 through 12 alone, over a quarter of students have experienced bullying. Electronic bullying has become a significant problem in the past decade. The ubiquity of hand-held and other devices affords bullies constant access to their prey, and harassment can often be carried out anonymously."

Bullying on social media is like bullying on steroids to a Gen-Xer or a Baby Boomer. Periodic bullying in a parking lot behind the school with few participants is very different than the relentless bullying that can occur on social media involving a much larger audience. A few years ago, I was tasked with responding to a shooting threat in a middle school. I conducted some groups with the kids to help them process the incident, and when we got to the bottom of it, we discovered that it was about bullying. I sat and listened to the kids in the group and was really concerned about their emotional health. Imagine trying to focus in a classroom under these conditions. I worked with these kids to change the group norm by empowering a couple of participants in the group who were natural leaders. Some of the kids in the classroom had been aligned with the bully in order to be popular, and some of the kids were aligned with him out of fear. The leaders, by being assertive with their thoughts and feelings, were able to inspire the rest of the group to abandon their allegiance with the bully. Talk about emotional intelligence! It was amazing for me to see these kids, many of whom didn't feel safe and secure, stand up as a group to the bully in the classroom.

Here are some tips for coaching your child to deal with bullying:

- Encourage your child to block bullies on cell phones and other forms of social media.

- Have them talk to a teacher or another authority figure at school.

- Encourage your child to travel in pairs.

- Teach and encourage assertiveness skills.

- Regularly check in with your child to see if they have been subject to bullying.

- Consider enrolling your child in a social skills training group.

Challenge Discussion # 4: Vaping Epidemic

Dr. Twenge reports that teens are drinking less and smoking marijuana more. We will likely see a rise in marijuana use as recreational use becomes legal across the U.S. The most concerning trend around substance use currently is the vaping epidemic. As Health and Human Services Secretary Alex Azar stated in a briefing, "We have never seen use of any substance by America's young people rise this rapidly. This is an unprecedented challenge." The tobacco companies are sly in their tactics by marketing nicotine to kids that is flavored like candy. When the kids reach later adolescence, they become addicted to nicotine and ingest it through vaping. These devices are dangerous because of the method of ingestion. The device enables the user to ingest very large amounts of nicotine that cross the blood-brain barrier extremely fast. Evidence is coming out that these devices have been linked to cardiovascular problems and seizures. Our task as parents is to educate our children on the dangers of vaping and foster prevention strategies such as the ones discussed in Jack's case study involving natural consequences and diversion.

Challenge Discussion # 5: Depression and Anxiety

In Chapter 3, I discussed the sharp increase in anxiety and depression experienced among our iGen kids. In my practice, when a client exhibits symptoms of depression or anxiety, I make an assessment to determine the root cause. In some cases, the cause appears to be a biological or neurological issue requiring medication. In other cases, the root cause may be situational or environmental, requiring therapy or coaching. Occasionally, the client needs both. From my perspective, the root cause of the sharp increase in mental health problems that are experienced by our iGen kids is environmental. I strongly believe that the technology boom is the culprit. Depression and anxiety affect teens regardless of gender, social background, income level, or other achievements. Common risk factors are:

- Family history of depression and anxiety; between 20 to 50 percent of teens with depression or anxiety have a family member who suffers from depression/anxiety or another mental health disorder.
- Experiencing trauma, abuse, or long-term illness or disability.
- Being bullied.
- Excessive screen time.
- Previous episodes of depression/anxiety.
- GLBTQIA children that get harassed by other kids in school for their sexual orientation.
- When a friend commits suicide.
- Addiction to drugs or alcohol.

Signs and symptoms of depression are as follows:

- Persistent feelings of sadness, irritability, or tension.
- Loss of interest in usual activities or hobbies.
- A change in appetite with a significant weight loss or gain.
- A change in sleeping patterns, such as difficulty sleeping, early morning awakening, or sleeping too much.
- Restlessness or feeling slowed down.
- Decreased ability to make decisions or concentrate.
- Feelings of worthlessness, hopelessness, or guilt.
- Thoughts of suicide or death.

Signs and symptoms of anxiety are as follows:

- Excessive worry occurring more days than not for at least 6 months.
- Difficulty controlling worries.
- Restlessness or feeling keyed up or on edge.
- Being easily fatigued.
- Difficulty concentrating or mind going blank.
- Irritability.
- Muscle Tension.
- Sleep disturbance.

If you believe your child is experiencing depression or anxiety, you have options. A good starting point is to meet and talk with your family doctor. She or he may refer you to a psychiatrist for medication or a mental health professional for therapy. If it is determined that these options are not necessary, you may wish to enlist the assistance of a coach or mentor.

Challenge Discussion #6: Teen Suicide

I received a call a few years ago to provide psycho-educational support to a high school that experienced a teen suicide. Three months prior, as a parent with a high school teenager, my community experienced a tragic teen suicide. Most of us have been touched by teen suicide in one way or another, and we all grieve when children in our communities decide to take their life. Our children's sense of security can be threatened when they lose a close friend or acquaintance so abruptly and to suicide. The distress reaction in schools often runs high, with so many kids fearful and grieving together. Administrators seeking out my help reported a significant increase in student hospitalizations following the suicide in their school.

Suicide is the third leading cause of death for children and young adults between the ages of ten and twenty-four years old. There are an estimated twenty-five attempts for every one completed suicide, and the risk increases dramatically when there are firearms in the home. Overdose, using over-the-counter prescription and nonprescription medicine, is a common method for attempting and completing suicide. Teen girls think about and attempt suicide twice as often as boys. They tend to overdose on drugs and cut themselves, whereas teen boys die by suicide four times more often than girls. Boys are also prone to using more violent methods, such as firearms, hanging, and jumping from heights.

The impact following a suicide depends on how close our children were to the child who died, or whether they were exposed to the trauma of witnessing distressing scenes. Feelings of guilt and anger are particularly pertinent to survivors. Kids may feel guilty for things they said or didn't say to their classmate who passed away. As parents, it is important to assure them that it was not their fault, but rather a decision made by someone who was not well.

Parents, if you are struggling emotionally, it is important to get help for yourself so that you are in a place to support your children. Talking to adults and keeping in touch with other parents is helpful. You may want to seek out counseling support if you are having a hard time helping your children.

Here are some tips for supporting your teen:

- It is OK to express your feelings around them if they are not out of control.
- Your child may need to talk to you a lot about the details of the incident itself.
- Keep the door open for them to share and give them some space if they need it.
- If they witnessed the death or know intimately someone who witnessed the death, this, in itself, is traumatic, and they may require professional help.
- Try to arrange individual time to talk or to just be together.
- Sometimes teenagers talk more to their friends than their parents. Your question as to how they are feeling may bring anger as a response.
- Make sure that your teenagers know that they are not responsible for what the person who was not feeling well did.
- Encourage your teenager to go to the funeral or take part in any rituals to mark the life and death of the young person. Closure can be very healing.

To all affected by the loss of a child, friend, classmate, or community member; it is important to allow yourself time and ritual to grieve. As painful as it is to talk about or face when our community loses a child to suicide, it is important that we talk about it and support each other through our grief for the sake of healing. Here are some important points to know about grief:

- There are no right or wrong ways to experience grief.
- There is no secret method that will take grief away instantly.

- There are no rules to grief; everyone grieves differently.

- There is no time table for grief.

- Grief becomes easier to heal from as time passes.

- Counseling may help you through the grief process.

- Take all of the time and space you need to grieve in your own way for as long as it takes.

Chapter 6 Assignment: Over the course of the week, have one-on-one discussions with your child on each of these topics. Tell them what you have learned. Be curious and ask them for their thoughts. Write a few paragraphs in your journal about your discussions.

Chapter 7:
Step 4—Design an Alliance

Relationship Is Key

Throughout this book, I have been talking about emotional intelligence skills as being more important than being "book smart" for success in school. In the same way, your relationship with your child is more important than how skilled you are at coaching them. In the fields of mental health and coaching, it is well-established that the relationship between therapist and client is what keeps them engaged and moving forward. A therapist or coach can have all of the credentials in the world and fail miserably if they don't know how to connect with their client. Sometimes parents get frustrated with me in my work with teens. Their child will tell them something like, "I like Dr. Hoy; we have some good talks and sometimes we listen to music." Then, I might receive a phone call from an angry dad who says something like, "My kid can listen to music or play games anywhere. Why am I paying for this?!" I tell him that it is a way for me to connect with your child so that they feel safe with me and gain trust.

Christopher was a 15-year-old client who came to me a few years ago. He was struggling greatly in school and at home. He had gone through several therapists prior to seeing me. His parents reported that he simply wouldn't talk with other therapists about his problems. He had a very short attention span and struggled with doing school work, completing chores, and following basic household rules. His parents punished him by grounding him in his room and taking the things away from him he most cared about. He loved music and had formed a small garage band with some kids from the neighborhood. However, his parents took away any access to music-practice time with friends, radio, television, computer, cell phones, and his guitar. This was an example of authoritarian parenting gone awry. The more his parents tried to control his behavior through harsh punishment, the more withdrawn, sullen, and defiant Christopher became. Our first few sessions were challenging to say the least. From his perspective, I was just another adult trying to tell him what to do. He responded to my inquiries with one-word answers, shrugs, and grunts. I had to find a different way to communicate with him. I asked him what bothered him the most about his parents. "They're always taking away my music!" he blurted. This gave me a clue about how to connect with him. I began to engage him in discussions about music. He came alive and educated me on a variety of different genres. I learned the difference between pop, hip hop, and rap. We began taking turns showing each other music videos that we liked on my computer. This was the beginning of our alliance. After a few weeks, I introduced structure and limits to our sessions. I explained that while I enjoyed him and the music, we had some work to do. By that point, we had established enough trust and safety in our relationship, that he was willing to negotiate with me. We then came to an agreement: he could play a song he liked at the beginning and the end of the session, and in between, he would talk about things he was struggling with like grades, school, and his frustration with his parents. Eventually, he brought music into the sessions that related to his life. That's when things really began to turn around for him.

In a sense, it was easier for me to establish an alliance with this young man than it was for his parents. I had no past history with him. His parents, on the other hand, had a history of conflicts and power struggles going back several years. They had significant work to do around repairing relationship damage and re-establishing their alliance. In order to facilitate this, I got the parents involved in the therapy. I began by validating their efforts and frustrations. I assured them that I was well aware of how difficult it is to raise teens. I had them bring in and share photo albums of them as a family growing up. I asked them to tell me what their happiest moments were with Christopher. As they shared stories about their son, they softened and were much more open about their feelings. They were able to connect with their deep love for him and identify that, behind their anger, was worry and fear for his future. As I got to know them better and they became more comfortable with me, they shared some of their shortcomings and struggles. We laughed together about how sometimes, as parents, we need to get over ourselves. They realized that they had very high expectations for Christopher and that much of their fear was about not wanting to look bad as parents. I then led them into a discussion about what they liked about Christopher and what his strengths were. "He can be really affectionate and he has a good sense of humor," said Dad. Mom added that he was a good musician. This opened Dad up to talk about his love of music and how he could identify with Christopher. I shared with Dad how I had connected with Christopher in sessions around music and encouraged him to do the same.

We were then ready to meet as a family. I facilitated a dialogue between Christopher and his parents, wherein they were able to take responsibility for the past mistakes they had made with him. As his parents modeled this behavior, Christopher became less defiant and began to take responsibility for his own mistakes. This cleaned the slate and set the stage for a new beginning. It was like hitting a "reset" button. From there, I led Christopher's parents into "rally" mode. I pointed out that the next few years were an opportunity for them to really have a huge impact, not only on his future but also on their long-term relationship with him. I coached them to think of themselves as cheerleaders first and disciplinarians second. This perspective shift was transformational for them. They became energized and began to redirect their efforts towards what was going right in his life. Unchained from their rigid expectations for him, they became excited about the possibility of moving forward. They began going to his neighborhood pick-up softball games. Dad occasionally substituted in for other players who couldn't make the games while Mom brought her fold-out chair and sat on the sidelines cheering them both on. His parents began to allow Christopher to invite his bandmates over to their garage for practice times. Eventually, the band invited Dad to sit in on a session and he taught them a Ramones song!

Although we made good progress, we weren't out of the woods. There were still disciplinary issues; after all, Christopher was only 15-years-old. I provided education to the parents on the parenting styles previously outlined in chapter 5. I coached them to adopt the Authoritative style as opposed to the Authoritarian style they had been using. They were able to continue to maintain high standards for school attendance and behavior without "keeping him down" with harsh punishment. Christopher was given space to bounce around, make mistakes, and learn from natural consequences within a container of safety created by his parents. When Christopher overslept and missed a class, instead of grounding him and taking away his music, his parents encouraged him to talk with his teacher about how to make up the class. His teacher required him to come into school on a Saturday morning and write a short paper on the topic of the class he missed. When natural consequences weren't readily available, they used logical consequences. For example, when Christopher came home an hour past curfew on a Friday evening, his parents made him come in an hour earlier the next time he went out. As for his homework, Christopher's mom began checking the school app every week, and if he had assignments missing, she would take him into her office with her on Saturdays. While she caught up on her paperwork, Christopher worked on his assignments. They would then take a break and have lunch together and discuss what he'd been working on, and she would praise him for his efforts. Sometimes they would take in a movie at the end of the day as a reward for his hard work. Gradually, Christopher began to experience more success in school. Success led to increased confidence and internal motivation. "It's so nice not to have to feel like I'm nagging him all the time," Mom said to me. At this point, the family was able to graduate from therapy.

Most of the case studies I have shared with you are more on the extreme side. Your situation may not be as intense or have all of the elements of Christopher and others like Jack. However, designing an alliance with your child, regardless of your situation, is the same. You need to take responsibility for your past mistakes without feeling like a failure as a parent, clean the slate, establish trust and safety in your relationship, identify a shared goal, and think of yourself as cheerleader first and disciplinarian second.

Taking Responsibility and Cleaning the Slate

Nobody's perfect; we all make mistakes. When my son was 15 years old, he told me he felt demoralized by my yelling. Consequently, I felt an intense guilt and sadness. I had to take a hard look at my behavior. I realized that, in response to his normal adolescent shenanigans, I had become controlling, unreasonable, and rigid. I took his behavior as an affront to my authority. I was surprised. There was a little voice in my head that said... "not *my* son—what will other people think of me?" I was so focused on myself and how I looked as a parent that I wasn't attuned to my son's needs. I was missing the big picture! My son's entire world was expanding—sports, girls, music, large classes, more homework, hormonal changes, and peer pressure. Rather than yell and try to control him, he needed me to walk beside him and help him navigate. His behavior was not about me. It was not an affront; it was a call to action. When I finally figured it out, I was able to acknowledge my mistakes and apologize.

Trust & safety

In my early work with Christopher, I was intentional about creating a safe space for him and developing trust. I led with authenticity. I was genuinely interested in him and he knew it. I listened much more than I talked. Although his parents had given me a large laundry list of complaints, I didn't judge, criticize, or tell him what to do. I let him know what he could expect of me. I would be honest and would show up every week. And if a problem arose with scheduling, I would call him and let him know. I set parameters; for example, we could have music at the beginning and end of our sessions, with problem discussions in the middle. I respected his pace and didn't try to push him to talk about issues he wasn't ready to address. After you clean the slate with your child, you will need to establish trust and safety in much the same way I did with Christopher.

Identify a Shared Goal

Having cleaned the slate and established trust and safety, our next task was to work on a shared goal. When I met with Christopher individually and asked him what his goals were for the next few years, he replied, "I want to have my own car and have the freedom to go and hang out with my friends." He wanted to be able to get some paid "gigs" on the weekends with his bandmates. "I want to get a dorm room at the University of Minnesota with my three best buds and study music. And, of course, I want a girlfriend." When I met with his parents and asked them what their goals for Christopher were for the next few years, Dad said, "He needs to get his grades up so he can get into a good business school." His mother wanted him to get into a profession where he could make enough money to live on his own and support a family. They were focused more on security, whereas Christopher's primary focus was on freedom.

Have you ever been involved in sports with your child? If so, you are probably well aware of how crazy some parents get when they watch their kids play. We absolutely lose all objectivity. It's understandable because of how much we love our kids. "Why isn't my kid pitching?! He's the best out there. She should be playing more! She's getting a raw deal! I'm going to talk to that coach!" Many parents who have kids in sports have played the same sport themselves when they were in high school. It is very common for us to want our kids to do better than we did. Unfortunately, "wants," can become expectations, and expectations can become demands. "You will make the varsity hockey team! You will not miss any practices! You will keep your grades up..." The unintended consequence of our deep love for our children can create a disconnect between our goals for them and their goals for themselves.

I brought Christopher and his parents in for a family session. I had each of them write down goals on sticky notes and put them up on butcher block paper on my office wall. I added some levity to the process by using many different colored sticky notes and encouraging them to dream big. I instructed them to do the exercise for 15 minutes non-stop and write down absolutely everything that came to their mind. By the end of the 15 minutes, my office wall had become a brightly-colored collage of hopes and wishes. From that collage, we identified two major themes: freedom and security. We grouped the sticky notes into these two categories on the wall. My job was to validate the importance of both themes of freedom and security. I educated Christopher's parents on how freedom and independence are very appropriate goals for a young man his age. I explained to Christopher that it was his parent's job to guide him, and sometimes that involves setting limits and having expectations. I then drew two overlapping circles on the butcher block paper, with one circle representing freedom and the other representing security. I had them determine which of their notes fit in the middle where the circles intersected, representing both security and freedom. The negotiations began. Christopher wanted music and his dad wanted business. The shared goals were that both parties valued higher education, financial independence, and social connections. I explained to Christopher's parents that passion creates movement, which was key for Christopher. When he gets into college, he may find something else he is passionate about and change his major. He may even find out that business is his passion. The point is that his parents needed to give him some room to explore and learn on his own.

Cheerleader First/Disciplinarian Second

In a private session with Christopher's parents, I told them, "it's like you have to be a cheerleader first and a disciplinarian second." Mom then brightened and said, "I was a cheerleader in high school!" I asked mom to give me a job description for a cheerleader. She explained, "you have to be able to create excitement with the fans for the team. You never lose faith; even when they are losing." She spoke about the importance of the cheer. "You have to cheer your team on and stay positive." I talked with mom about how I would grimace when I was in high school watching the cheerleaders doing a series of flips across the field and landing into the splits. Mom said, "oh yeah, we did all of that stuff." "In other words," I said, "you had to be very flexible." "Yes... for sure!" she exclaimed. I drew an analogy between cheerleading on a sports team and cheerleading for your child. I encouraged them to be excited for him and never lose faith; even when he is having a bad day. I coached them to praise him more for his efforts than the outcome and to celebrate any and every victory, no matter how small. Above all, I underscored the importance of being flexible and willing to bend.

Freedom to move and explore is very important for our teen children, however, it is crucial for parents to provide a safe container in which to do so. When working with parents to convey this message, I have them remember their child as a toddler learning to walk and move about. They take off, stop, look back at you, and decide whether to run to you or continue on. It can be perilous. Sometimes they fall down. This is a natural consequence of exploration. Often, you have to swoop in and rescue them from danger; like falling down a flight of stairs, or sticking a finger in a light socket. You may have to discipline them to keep them safe. This is how we provide containment for our toddlers. When children become teenagers, we revisit this stage in many ways. They need to explore and experiment with new behaviors. Sometimes it is perilous. "Falling down" for a teenager might look like getting detention for clowning around in the classroom or being embarrassed by a Snapchat post. These are examples of natural consequences. Sometimes, you have to swoop in and rescue them from danger, like going to parties, hanging out with older kids, and experimenting with alcohol. You may have to discipline them to keep them safe.

As discussed in Chapter 5, authoritative parenting has been found to produce the best results with kids. Kids whose parents choose this style get better grades. As you are designing your alliance with your child, let them know that you are adopting a coaching style that you have learned is one that will help them get good grades. This way, they will know you are working for their success, instead of trying to control them. If their grades are down, let them know that they can expect you to set limits on leisure activities. As they get back on track, you will ease up and allow them to spend time on other things they like to do. Set high expectations for school attendance and negotiate use of social media. I recommend you work with them towards staying away from their devices while they are studying, unless they are using them for school work. Give them some space during the week with reporting on status of assignments. Shoot for a check-in time once a week, at a time you both agree on. Talk with them about getting a job. Part-time work for teens has been found to improve grades because it helps kids get into a rhythm. Ask them what they need from you to help them improve school performance. Do the best you can in setting up a household environment conducive to learning. When they do well, it is more effective to praise them for their effort, rather than an outcome, such as getting a good grade on a test.

Sometimes as parents, we put the cart before the horse and try to get to the end goal too quickly. Building a strong alliance takes patience. Think of it as a process. Take time to make time. If you are unable to maintain a strong alliance with your child throughout this process, they will not be on board with you. A great way to connect is to find out what they like, or something they are good at, and take a genuine interest in it with them. You can expect that you will get some pushback throughout this process. That's what kids do. If you are feeling stressed out when they push back, they are going to feel the same way. Being stressed out all of the time reduces our ability to problem-solve. Try your best to avoid power-struggles and definitely choose your battles. If you get deadlocked on something and emotions are running high,

I recommend moving on to something else. Make sure you are fully present when you meet. Be authentic. When setbacks occur, focus on what you can do to move forward instead of spending most of your time on what didn't work. You can certainly build some fun into this process. Negotiate activities you can do together as rewards, like going out to movies or meals together. And whatever you do, don't give up. You are in this one hundred percent.

Chapter 7 Assignment: Gather a bunch of multicolored sticky notes and meet with your child. Take fifteen minutes to dream big and write down as many goals for your child as possible. Have your child do the same for him/herself. Find common themes, group them together, and determine where the intersection is. Identify one, two or three shared goals to be allied around moving forward.

Chapter 8:
Step 5—Lay a Solid Foundation

Good job! You have designed an alliance with your child. Let's make sure we have our feet under us. In this chapter, I am going to talk about the importance of foundational skills, not only for your child's success in school, but for the overall health of their generation. I am aware that you most likely know a great deal about time management, nutrition, sleep, and physical activity. However, just because we *know* what we need, doesn't mean we always *do* what we need. We stock our houses with healthy foods, provide comfy beds and an alarm clock, put a trampoline in the back yard, a basketball hoop in the driveway, and expect our kids to do the rest. The truth of the matter is, they are neither sleeping, exercising, eating right, or managing their time effectively. A record number of our iGen kids are in crisis. They are distracted to the point of ignoring critical foundational needs. Most of the distraction they are experiencing is preventable. At the risk of sounding like my grandfather: WE NEED TO GET OUR KIDS BACK TO THE BASICS!

Time Management

I recently interviewed fifty college students in five focus groups and asked them what they thought was the most stressful part of transitioning from high school to college. The hands-down response was "time management." One of the participants talked about feeling depressed after making a conscious choice to go down the "rabbit hole" of spending all night on her cell phone when she knew she was supposed to be studying. Another one talked about arriving late to class for exams and being so anxious she couldn't answer the test questions that she had studied for. Time management is not only linked to higher GPAs but it has also been shown to lower anxiety and reduce stress by creating a sense of control. Now is the time to get your child going on a time management plan. Here are some suggestions for getting started:

- *Time management tools.* Whether it's a planner that your teen writes everything in or an app that manages their schedule, help them find the tools that will work best. Talk about the importance of creating a schedule and using lists to prioritize time wisely.

- *Write down a schedule.* Teach your teen to schedule their day so they can set aside time for chores, homework, and other responsibilities. You can also encourage them to schedule free time.

- *Prioritize activities.* It's common for teens to run into conflicts in their schedules. Teach them how to prioritize activities based on values and commitments.

- *Develop routines.* Encourage your teen to establish routines, like doing chores right after school. Routines help teens stay on track and on task.

- *Set limits on electronics.* Negotiate a plan to help your child create healthy habits with cell phones and other digital devices.

- *Model good time management habits.* Be on time for your child and model punctuality by making it to appointments when scheduled. Demonstrate your ability to use time management habits to balance work, personal, and family life.

One of the biggest stressors reported by teens coming out of high school, is adjusting to the amount of studying they have to do in college. And many kids enter college unaware of how to properly prepare for exams. Here are some time management study tips to pass on to your high schooler to help prepare them for the rigors of college life:

1. Take good notes: Date each entry and keep notes from different classes separate from each other. Write down anything your instructor puts on the board. If the instructor took the time to write it out, then he or she considers it important. Try to take notes in outline form. The organization of ideas is as important as the content, especially when it comes to learning exam material.

2. Review your notes every day: Spend thirty minutes each evening going over notes from each class. Research shows that reviewing new material within twenty-four hours after hearing it increases your retention of that material significantly. Review material before each class to identify points of confusion and prepare you for asking questions.

3. Alternate study locations: Alternating study spaces is an effective way to retain information. Although you may have a favorite spot to study, research suggests that it is better to change locations. Memory is influenced by location, so changing your study locale increases the likelihood of remembering what you learned.

4. Get enough sleep: Sleep is essential when it comes to effective study. When you're tired, you think more slowly and tend not to retain as much information. If you want to get the most out of your study sessions, make sure you get enough sleep.

5. Use flashcards: Writing notes and definitions more than once will help imprint information in your memory. Write down important facts for a test and quiz yourself each day until you have mastered the material. Flashcards are convenient because they allow you to condense material and eliminate irrelevant information.

6. Join a study group: When working through a difficult problem set or assignment, a study group can prove invaluable. Dividing the work amongst your peers is also an effective method for reducing your workload and ensuring that you understand the material.

7. Don't immerse yourself in subject matter: Immersing yourself in a subject for long periods of time is less effective when it comes to memory retention than switching between topics. Take a break from each topic after thirty minutes and move on to another. You can come back to the topic after you have spent some time studying others. When you do revisit the topic, you will feel refreshed and ready to pick up where you left off.

8. Don't wait until the night before an exam to study: Cramming before an exam causes feelings of desperation and can lead to test anxiety. Instead, jot down a few ideas or facts that you want to have fresh in your mind before the test. Read through your list a few times when you get up in the morning and once again just before you take the exam. This kind of memory reinforcement not only improves your performance on the test, but also your long-term memory of the material.

9. College-level study requirements: In higher education, a well-established rule of thumb holds that students should devote two hours of study time for every hour of class time. Full-time students taking 15 credits can plan on studying 30 hours per week.

Sleep Hygiene

We are a sleep-deprived society! A recent report from the Centers for Disease Control estimated that over one-third of the adult population in the U.S. sleeps less than the recommended minimum of seven hours each night. And teens, who need just over nine hours of sleep a night, are the least likely of any age group to get sufficient rest. According to a survey from the National Sleep Foundation, about 87 percent of American high school students are chronically sleep-deprived. Sleep deprivation has been linked to increases in depression, suicide attempts, learning and behavior issues in school. Schools have established later start times for children as we have become aware that sufficient sleep is linked to higher grades. The biggest current-day contributors to lack of sleep, as you can probably guess, are from electronic devices: cell phones, television, MP3 players, texting, and video games. Teenagers naturally have a harder time sleeping at night because of a delay in the release of a hormone, melatonin, which is secreted when it is dark to induce sleep. Sleeping in close proximity to an electronic device that gives off light delays the release of melatonin. It's like throwing gas on a fire. Your child's sleep is not only disrupted by staying up late at night and using an electronic device, but by sleeping next to it. Below is a snapshot of some statistics from a survey done by Michigan Medicine from the University of Michigan, who polled parents about teen sleep disruption:

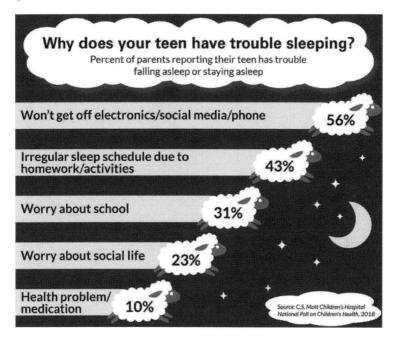

Fifty-six percent of parents reported teen sleep deprivation due to use of electronics and social media. Forty-three percent attributed irregular sleep to homework requirements and other activities, such as sports. Thirty-one percent said their kids often laid awake at night worrying about school. Twenty-three percent reported that their kids stayed up worrying about social lives, and 10 percent cited health problems as a cause for disrupted sleep. Below are a number of suggestions to help your teen have better sleep.

- *Ban electronics from the bedroom.* Use of electronics, including social media and cellphones, is the top reason parents cite for their teens' sleep troubles.

- *Charge cell phones elsewhere.* Make it a family rule to charge all devices in an isolated space to reduce temptation at bedtime. Many teens describe a sense of relief when their parents limit phone use because it takes away some of the pressure to keep up with peers on social media.

- *Maintain a regular sleep schedule.* Keeping a sleep schedule within an hour of what's usual helps to keep the sleep cycle in check. Sleeping in late on weekends doesn't make up for lost sleep.

- *Discourage afternoon naps.* Naps make it harder to fall asleep at night.

- *Don't procrastinate on big tasks.* Encourage getting homework done as soon as teens get home from school, or negotiate a short break before they begin.

- *Stick to sleep-friendly bedtime routines.* All stimulation should be minimized. Keep the lights low and active pets out of the bedroom. Some kids like to use music to relax and wind down; however, this may actually keep their brains stimulated.

- *Limit caffeine.* Discourage energy drinks, which tend to have much higher levels of caffeine than tea or coffee. Discourage the use of caffeinated drinks later than lunchtime to prevent sleep disruption.

- *Talk with your doctor about melatonin.* Teens naturally have a harder time getting to sleep at night. Melatonin may be helpful.

Nutrition

Just as sleep has been proven to help teens get better grades, so has attention to proper nutrition. Eating breakfast each morning has positive effects on brain function. Kids who eat breakfast have better concentration during school hours than kids who skip the morning meal. Nationally, 60 percent of American teens skip eating breakfast on a daily basis. According to pediatrician Dr. William Sears, children who eat breakfast in the morning before school participate more in class discussions, are better able to handle complex problems, and get better grades. In particular, a breakfast meal containing a balance of protein and complex carbohydrates boosts school performance for your child throughout the day. Complex carbohydrates and proteins make your child's brain alert and contribute to better learning. Here are some suggestions for a healthy breakfast:

- Instant oatmeal with fruits and nuts.
- Higher calcium, lower fat dairy foods.
- Whole-grain cereal with dried fruits, nuts, and low-fat milk or soy milk.
- Egg breakfasts with a minimum of fat.
- High protein yogurt with fruits.
- Whole wheat bread with peanut butter or cheese.
- Fruit salad with cottage cheese.
- A shake blended with yogurt, milk or soy milk, and fruits.

If your teen isn't hungry first thing in the morning, be sure to pack a breakfast that they can eat a little later on the bus or between classes, such as fresh fruit, cereal, nuts, or half a peanut butter and banana sandwich. Sandwiches are easy to make and easy for kids to take along and eat later on. Teens typically need more calories due to rapid growth and development. Specifically, boys need an average of 2800 calories per day, while girls need an average of 2200 calories. Protein bars have several benefits and drawbacks. For example, they are a better option than fast food, concession stand, or vending machine food choices, and they are a better option than skipping a meal completely during the day. If you are going to use protein bars as nutritional choices for your kids, make sure you read the labels to find out what is in them. Some are rich in nutrients and some are more like candy bars with sugars and unhealthy fats. Others contain extra un-needed carbohydrates intended for endurance athletes.

In 2011, the USDA replaced the food pyramid with a nutritional guide called "My Plate." It depicts a place setting with a plate and glass divided into five food groups: fruits, grains, vegetables, protein, and dairy.

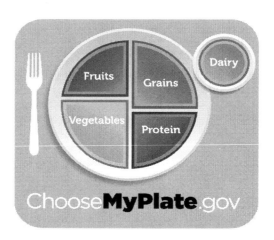

Visit the USDA web site (ChooseMyPlate.Gov) with your child to teach them about nutrition, using the plate as a guide for meal planning. The Centers for Disease Control report that teens consume significantly fewer fruits and vegetables required by dietary guidelines. Girls should eat 1.5 cups of fruit and 2.5 cups of vegetables daily, while boys should eat two cups of fruit and three cups of vegetables. A cup is the equivalent of one medium-sized apple or eight strawberries. Health care experts are now pondering the addition of water intake to the My Plate Guide. Statistics from a National Health and Nutrition Survey indicate that most American teens aren't drinking enough water and are mildly dehydrated. Teens, in general, report drinking little fluids of any kind overall. Dehydration (even mild), negatively impacts energy level, mood, and learning. Teenagers should consume roughly two to three quarts or 1.7 to 3.3 liters of water a day.

Let's take a minute to talk about junk food. In a 2015 article in the New York times, statistics from the Centers for Disease Control reveal that American teens consume 16.9 percent of their calories from junk food, such as Hamburgers, French Fries, and Pizza. On any given day, researchers calculated that 34.5 percent of children and adolescents aged 2-19 years-old take in 25 percent of their calories from junk food. And as you can imagine, junk food consumption leads to obesity. An article in US News reported the following, "In the United States, almost 38 percent of adults are obese and about 18.5 percent of kids under 19 years old are obese. "Obesity leads to heart disease, diabetes, high blood pressure and cholesterol, bone and joint problems, and asthma." Severe obesity has become so prevalent and dangerous among youth that the American Academy of Pediatrics now recommends that bariatric (weight loss) surgery be considered as a safe treatment option for children and teens. As a health professional, it is hard for me to believe that a surgery once considered a last-ditch resort for adults with morbid obesity is entering the mainstream as an acceptable treatment for young people! According to a large study in the US News & World Report, there is a positive correlation between watching junk food ads and consuming foods that are high in salt, sugar, and fat. The bottom line is that kids who watch more ads tend to eat more junk. Here goes my grandpa's voice again: TURN OFF THE TV! GET AWAY FROM THAT COMPUTER! THOSE ADS WILL BRAINWASH YOU!

Advertisements and social media glorify eating unhealthy foods, while at the same time celebrating unrealistic body images. We are barraged by pictures of skinny women and muscular men as ideal body types. Teens searching for identity are particularly susceptible to these messages. To this end, they can become vulnerable to buying in to the fad diet craze. Fad diets can be dangerous because they are not balanced or sustainable. Signs of a fad diet are:

- Promise of a huge weight loss in a short period of time. For example, "Drop 10 pounds in one week, guaranteed."

- Claims that the diet works with no exercise needed.

- Certain foods are never allowed.

- Foods are called "good" or "bad."

- Special foods are needed that are hard to find or can only be bought in certain shops.

Fad diets can lead to eating disorders among young people. The National Eating Disorder Association (NEDA) has reported that eating disorders have been increasing steadily since the 1950s.

In her book, *Understanding Teen Eating Disorders: Warning Signs, Treatment Options and Stories of Courage,* Mary Tantillo identifies the following behaviors that may indicate your child is struggling with an eating disorder:

1. BODY INSECURITY: Negative or obsessive thoughts about body size or shape. Persistent worries or complaints about being fat or the need to lose weight.

2. EXCESSIVE EXERCISE: Obsessive about getting daily exercise. Exercises even when injured, tired, or sick.

3. FEAR OF EATING IN FRONT OF OTHERS: Avoids situations that include eating in front of others or in public. Makes excuses about not being able to eat with friends or family.

4. VICARIOUS PLEASURE IN OTHERS' EATING: Prepares elaborate meals for others but rarely eats what is made.

5. CHANGES IN APPEARANCE: Significant loss, gain, or fluctuation in weight. Puffy cheeks due to swollen salivary glands. Hair loss, dry hair or skin, or excessive facial or body hair.

6. PHYSIOLOGICAL CHANGES: Develops unusual sleep patterns and a sensitivity to cold, feels faint or tired, menstrual cycles stop or become irregular.

7. EXCESSIVELY RESTRICTING FOODS: Considers certain foods or food groups completely off-limits. Preoccupied with dieting, fat grams, or calories. Equates eating with self-control. Lack of interest in food.

8. EXCESSIVE FEAR: Avoids certain foods for fear of choking or purging. This applies to those suffering from severe restrictive food intake disorder.

9. OVERCONSUMPTION OF FOOD: Frequently consumes very large amounts of food and seems out of control during these binge-eating episodes. Shows a pattern of eating when not hungry and eats to the point of discomfort.

10. PURGING: May compensate for eating through vomiting, laxative or diuretic abuse, or other substances. Leaves the table soon after the meal to purge.

11. SECRETIVE EATING: Large amounts of food disappear over short periods of time. Presence of wrappers or containers that might indicate secret consumption of large quantities of food.

12. EATING RITUALS: Obsessively cuts food into small pieces or arranges food to create the appearance of actually eating, while little or no food is consumed.

13. ISOLATION: Withdraws from usual friends and activities. Isolates and gets moody especially after eating. May make continual excuses about not being able to eat with peers.

If you are seeing signs and symptoms of an eating disorder, take them seriously. The National Eating Disorder Association (NEDA) is a great resource for help and support in your area. Their helpline number is: 800-931-2237 and their website can be found at: https://www.nationaleatingdisorders.org/help-support/contact-helpline A good starting point is to make an appointment with your family doctor.

Physical Activity

Good news! Physical activity will increase your child's grade point average. According to scientific research reported by the California College of San Diego, exercise improves memory and information processing functions. If practiced on a regular basis, it can boost GPAs. Here's how it works. When kids exercise, carbohydrates are broken down into glucose, which are sugars. Glucose is literally food for the brain. Regular exercise creates a storage of glucose in two parts of the brain critical for memory and learning—the hippocampus and the neocortex. Cardiovascular exercise is particularly effective for increasing glycogen stores and enlarging the brain. In essence, exercise feeds the brain and makes it larger and smarter. Adults need about 150 minutes of exercise per week. The Centers for Disease Control report that only 23 percent of adults follow this recommendation. Teens need about one hour of physical activity almost every day. Unfortunately, only three in ten teens meet these guidelines and have been compared in research to be consistent with sixty-year-olds in terms of exercise habits. We have to get our kids moving! It doesn't have to be so intense that it turns them off. You want to find something they like that keeps them moving most every day. Here are some tips for encouraging healthy exercise for your child:

- **Start with small changes:** For those who are not in the habit of exercising, here is what I know. It is often more the *thought* of doing it beforehand that demotivates a person than actually doing the exercise. For example, your child gets home from school and wants to play video games. You suggest he/she exercise and they bristle. Negotiate with them. They can control how long and intensely they exercise. It may be only 10 minutes. They are likely to be more motivated because they know it won't take long. What usually happens is they forget about the time, because it feels good. The fact that they know they are in control is liberating. Consistency (e.g., six to seven days every week), even if only 10 minutes, is most important for developing and sustaining a routine.

- **It is more effective to make it fun than intense:** It is easy to associate exercise with work or strain on the body. If you can find activities involving movements that are fun, kids are more likely to engage. For example, some kids don't necessarily like to "exercise," but enjoy being outdoors. Canoeing, biking, hiking, nature walks, or swimming may be options.

- **Focus on health, not weight loss:** Exercising for weight loss is OK, however, it can also lead to negative associations. Educate your child on the mental and physical health benefits of exercise to change from a negative to a positive mindset. Physically-active kids have bigger brains, live longer lives, and are generally happier.

- **Find the right activity:** Experiment. Try something new each week. Talk to your child and find out what they like. Remember, if it is fun, it doesn't feel like work!

- **Find activities you can do together:** It doesn't matter how old your kids are. There are always things to do together that are not only fun and physically healthy, but a great way to connect with each other. Take turns as a family choosing different activities.

- **Model good habits for your child:** My fondest childhood memories are of running with my father. I watched him quit smoking at 40-years-old and take up running. He ran daily and got me interested in running races. To this day, I exercise regularly and model good physical health habits for my kids.

Chapter 8 Exercise: Go through this material and negotiate structures in your daily lives to attend to these very important foundational skills. Write them down for weekly review. Parents, I strongly encourage you to participate alongside your child.

Yay! We have finally made it to emotional intelligence! Chapter 9 is very important and is much more detailed than all others. Rather than waiting until the end of the chapter to give suggestions for assignments, I have provided options for you to consider throughout. Pick and choose the ones that best suit you.

Chapter 9:
Step 6—Infuse Emotional Intelligence Skills

There has long been a debate in the fields of business and education about what factors contribute more to success in school, at work, and in life. It has been coined as the "IQ vs. EQ" debate. IQ is short for intelligence quotient, while EQ stands for emotional intelligence. You or your child may have taken an IQ test at some point in your lives to assess your intelligence levels. Here's what an IQ test measures:

- **Visual and spatial processing:** your ability to mentally manipulate 3D objects.

- **Knowledge of the world:** general knowledge about pop culture and history.

- **Fluid reasoning:** analysis of patterns and puzzles.

- **Working memory and short-term memory:** memory recall.

- **Quantitative reasoning:** the application of basic mathematics skills to the analysis and interpretation of real-world quantitative information.

The basis behind traditional IQ tests are to measure genetic potential for learning and are believed to be unchangeable, for the most part, throughout our lifetime. In essence, the presumption is that we are all born with a level of intelligence that remains the same throughout our life span and dictates our success.

Here's an example of what an EQ (emotional intelligence) test measures:

- **Self-awareness:** how aware we are of our feelings in any given moment.

- **Self-management:** how well we manage our emotions.

- **Social skills:** how well we relate to others.

- **Empathy:** how well we understand the experience of others.

The concept of emotional intelligence has been around for a very long time. Dr. Daniel Goleman, whom I referred to earlier in chapter 6, has done groundbreaking research in demonstrating how important these skills are for success in the workplace. In his research, he sought to discover characteristics that set star performers apart from others. And it wasn't the people with the highest IQs. IQ has been found to contribute to only 20% of an individual's success in life. Your child will be required to have a certain set of intelligence skills (IQ) to perform tasks unique to the job they choose. For example, a surgeon has to have highly-developed visual-spatial skills or they won't be able to perform the basic functions of their job. Why, however, does one surgeon become a lead administrator or chief of surgery in front of another very intelligent peer? Through his research, Dr. Goleman found that people with highly developed emotional intelligence skills are the ones who get promotions and become leaders.

The same holds true in education. It is now common knowledge that kids with higher degrees of emotional intelligence not only get better grades but also stay in school longer. Would you be surprised to learn that positivity is a better predictor of college students' first year GPA's than SAT scores? Hard to believe, isn't it? It's true. The three strongest predictors of making it through college to graduation are being socially responsible, learning to manage impulses, and having empathy for others. These are all characteristics of an emotionally-intelligent student. Steven Stein and colleagues, in their book, *The Student EQ Edge: Emotional Intelligence And Your Academic And Personal Success*, present studies that highlight the correlation between emotional intelligence, grade point averages, and school success. You should see the look on parents' faces in my practice when I talk about this. It can be hard to wrap your head around, and it is at the core of the message that I am trying to convey to you in this book. Your child's success in high school or college is not just about being "book smart." By book smart, I am talking about how well they are able to learn and score on tests in school.

More than two decades ago, the Collaborative for Academic, Social, and Emotional Learning (CASEL) defined the term, Social and Emotional Learning (SEL). SEL is about integrating emotional intelligence skills into school systems. As published in the Journal of Child Development, CASEL produced a series of cutting-edge results in 2017 from a meta-analysis they conducted on 213 social and emotional learning programs in schools. The study found that approximately 50 percent of kids enrolled in SEL programs had better achievement scores and almost 40 percent showed improved grade point averages. These programs were also linked to lowered suspension rates, increased school attendance, and reduced disciplinary problems. Based on 8 studies that measured academic performance, the researchers showed that students exposed to emotional intelligence programs were an average of thirteen percentile points higher than their non-SEL peers. Conduct problems, emotional distress, and drug use were all significantly lower for students exposed to SEL programs. The evidence is overwhelming. Emotional intelligence is extremely important for success in school. Unlike traditional measures of IQ, emotional intelligence (EQ) doesn't remain the same over our life span. It is heavily impacted by our environment and our interaction with others. Good news. There is much we can do as parents, teachers, coaches, and mentors to help our children raise their EQs!

The Neuro of Emotional Intelligence

Before I explain the skill sets involved in emotional intelligence, I want to help you understand EQ on a deeper level. Below is the figure I presented in chapter 6.

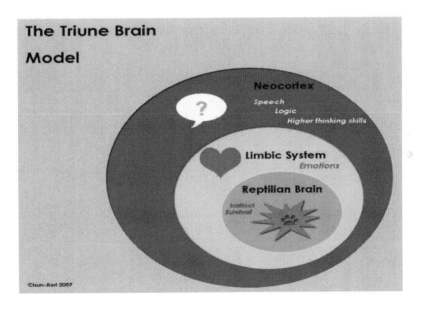

The brain grows and develops from the bottom up, beginning with the most primitive instinctual reptilian brain, to the mid-brain, which is the limbic system. The limbic system is responsible for assigning and managing emotions based on how we experience the environment around us. The outer part of the brain, the neocortex, is responsible for higher-order thinking skills. There is a pathway of electrical signals beginning in the lower brain that travels up through the limbic system to the outer brain. When our kids are sorting out feelings and deciding how to act on them, there is a complex interplay between the emotional and rational parts of the brain. Think of the emotional part of the brain as the feeling part, and the rational part of the brain as the thinking part. Kids with high emotional intelligence skills are able to sort out thoughts and feelings and make good decisions in the moment. Imagine your teen in a group of friends at a party, feeling happy and excited to be with each other, when one of their peers asks them to do something risky, like jump off of the roof of the garage into a pool in the back yard. Your child is caught up in the heat of the moment and feels intense peer pressure to make the jump. There is a split second of time where their brain has to process the moment and make a decision to jump.

The more we teach emotional intelligence skills, and the more our children practice them, the stronger the neural connections become between the rational and emotional parts of the brain. There is a term in neurobiology called "plasticity." Plasticity is a measure of how our brains adapt to change. This is similar to lifting weights. The more we lift, the more muscle fiber we develop and the physically stronger we become. The more our kids practice emotional intelligence skills, the more efficiently the emotional and rational parts of their brain communicate with each other, resulting in better decision making, such as deciding that jumping off of the roof of the garage into the pool is a bad idea.

Neural communication not only takes place through pathways in the brain, but between people. We now know through the field of neuroscience that we have a certain percentage of neurons in our brains that imitate each other, known as mirror neurons. We literally "bluetooth" with each other. Our neural connection with our kids is important for healthy brain development and is very much a part of teaching emotional intelligence. Parents and teens need to sync more with each other and much less with wireless devices. We can teach our kids very powerful lessons through modeling. Think about a high school baseball coach who is trying to teach kids the fundamentals of fielding a ground ball and throwing it to first base. He goes into detail about a complex set of movements and body positioning that have to take place to be successful. "Athletic position-move your feet-soft hands-solid base." When it is time for the kids to try, he gets frustrated. "Don't you remember what I told you! Move your feet! Soft hands!" The following week, he brings in a recent high school graduate who is playing college baseball. He hits balls to him as his players sit on the bench and watch. They observe him as he crouches down into an athletic position, feet shoulder-width apart, knees slightly bent, glove to the ground. They see him quickly move his feet to get in front of the ball. The ball is moving fast and bouncing hard as it comes towards him. Moving with the energy of the ball like a martial artist practicing Tai Chi, he scoops it up, and with one fluid motion, makes a perfect throw to first base. The kids on the bench go wild. "Did you see that! OMG that was cool! He's really smooth." When the kids begin to field ground balls, the coach notices that they perform much better than last week. They had learned and internalized fundamental skills by watching and identifying with the older, more experienced player. When our children witness us using skills like managing emotions, socializing, or demonstrating empathy for others, we are activating and strengthening their neural networks, which are involved in developing these skills.

Our "bluetooth" connection with our kids is wonderful. We use it to teach thousands of lessons, from patty cake and peekaboo, to how to use a spoon, to potty training, to minding your manners in public. As exciting as it is to know about the power of mirror neurons, it is important to understand that there is a dark side. Have you ever heard a toddler blurt out a swear word? You are surprised to hear such profanity come out of a little person's mouth. You wonder, "Where did they learn that?" When our kids are exposed to environments with negativity, such as extensive yelling and hostility, we are building these neural networks as well.

When I work with families, I often have to intervene and change the energy in the room. Emotions can become contagious and take over. I'll have a mother and daughter in my office getting into heated arguments. I feel the energy in my body, and for a split second, have the urge to raise my voice along with them. There can be a diminishing point of marginal returns on emotions. I encourage emotional expression as a way of gaining mutual understanding, resolving conflicts, and deepening connections. However, sometimes, when emotions get too high, we get stuck in "limbic lava" and meaningful communication shuts down. If sustained for long periods of time, it can become abusive and damaging. As a therapist, I have to sense when this is happening and change the energy. Parents, you can do this too. If your child is upset and having a hard time calming down, it is extremely helpful to find a way to change the energy. It might mean taking a time out from the conversation with a commitment to revisiting later. Model deep breathing and modulate your voice tone. A calm presence is much more powerful than words in helping children regulate emotions.

Self-Awareness

Self-awareness is the foundational building block to all of the other emotional intelligence skills discussed in this book. Self-aware teens are able to identify feelings in any given moment and act in accordance. When our children are unable to correctly identify feelings, they can make mistakes with coping behaviors. And often, teens struggle to separate thoughts from feelings. I have had kids in my office who report feeling like a "loser," or "stupid," or "like punching someone in the mouth." These are not feelings, but rather self-judgments and thoughts that can lead to responses that escalate problems. Feelings are emotional states that take place in the body. Let's go back to my example of the child standing on top of the garage needing to make a split-second decision about jumping into the pool. He comes into my office with stitches in his forehead and bumps and bruises all over his body. I ask him how he was feeling before he jumped and he responds to me by saying, "I felt like I had to jump because some of my buddies already had." I go on to ask, "How could you tell you were feeling like you had to jump? Where did you experience it in your body?" He says, "What do you mean? I felt like I had to jump!" "Let's revisit that moment on top of the garage," I say. "What was happening in your chest? Was your heart beating fast, or slow?" He tells me his heart was pounding. "How was your breath? Was it deep and slow, or was it shallow and fast?" "I was holding my breath," he explains. "And what was happening in your stomach?" "It was all jittery and a little bit sick." I give him a list of emotional states to consider: happy, sad, mad, scared, embarrassed, excited, and guilty. "Scared and embarrassed," he explains. "Ok, so you felt embarrassed and scared." "Yes," he says. I then help him tease out the thoughts connected to each of these emotional states. Embarrassment led to the thought: "everyone is going to laugh at me if I don't jump. They're going to talk about me being a wimp on Instagram." The thought connected to the fear was: "I'm not sure if I can make the jump and I could get hurt." I work to help him understand that when his brain misinterprets his feelings, he limits his options. "There is no such thing as feeling like you have to jump," I tell him. You feel embarrassed and scared, and your brain comes up with only one option, so you jump. This is an example of how kids can make poor choices when they are not aware of the difference between what they are thinking and how they are feeling.

Triggers

In addition to being clear about thoughts, feelings, and the difference between the two, another very important aspect of self-awareness is knowing your "triggers." A trigger is an event or situation that can lead to a stress reaction. Triggers are usually caused by something in the surrounding environment or by another person's actions. Our children are often unaware of their triggers and need help to manage them. Below are some of the most common triggers for high school students, most of which were mentioned previously in chapter 4.

- **Academic stress:** Exams and deadlines can trigger anxiety; especially if your child hasn't developed good time management skills.

- **Social media:** Comparing themselves to others, experiencing harassment, humiliation, or rejection from peers on social media can be extremely disturbing for teens.

- **Family problems:** Divorce, separation, marital problems, sibling disputes, and financial struggles all contribute to anxiety which can make it hard to focus on school.

- **World events:** Kids have access to world news 24/7 and can become easily overwhelmed by hearing about school shootings, acts of terrorism, or natural disasters.

- **Traumatic events:** Death of family members, car accidents, sickness, and enduring emotional or physical abuse is very stressful for kids.

- **Significant life changes:** Moving, starting at a new school, divorce, separation, and the blending of families can be a significant source of stress.

- **Peer pressure:** By nature, teens have an intense need to fit in with peers. Negative peer pressure can result in poor choices around substance use, sexual behaviors, and how they treat others (e.g., bullying behaviors).

- **Parental pressure:** As parents, if we are constantly putting pressure on our kids to perform in every aspect of life, we can inadvertently be setting them up for failure.

Self-defeating Behaviors

As we become more self-aware, we not only gain insight into our thoughts, feelings, and sources of stress, but also our default patterns of coping behavior. A default pattern of behavior is something we have learned to do to cope with stress that becomes problematic. As Doctor Phil commonly asks his clients, "How's that working for you?" Jack's case study, as mentioned in chapter 4, exemplifies how kids can get stuck in self-defeating patterns of behavior as a result of stress. He struggled greatly, not only with his parent's divorce, but also with their ongoing co-parenting disagreements. He became angry and pessimistic and began getting into physical altercations. He got so far behind in school that he gave up trying. As a member of the hockey team, he violated substance abuse policies, knowing that it could jeopardize his playing status. When he felt safe enough to identify and express his true feelings, he became aware of how he had been coping by engaging in some very self-defeating behaviors. Here are some common self-defeating behaviors teens engage in. Take a look at the list below and see if any of the behaviors pertain to your child.

- Smoking and vaping.
- Skipping classes at school.
- Not asking for help.
- Avoiding self-care.
- Substance abuse.

- Hanging out with kids who get in trouble.

- Giving up.

- Not studying.

- Procrastinating.

- Yelling and screaming.

- Not listening.

- Bullying.

Now that you are aware of what a self-defeating behavior is, you may want to think of what some of your own default patterns are. We all have them. One of mine, for example, is to ignore self-care when I get involved in a big project. My faulty thinking is: "I don't have time for anything else." These thoughts can backfire on me as I get tired and my creativity and productivity go down. A good way to broach this subject with your child is to explain that everyone has self-defeating patterns of behavior, including you. You can start the discussion by disclosing one of yours. The more you normalize discussions about thoughts, feelings, sources of stress, and self-defeating behaviors, the more open your child will be to talking about theirs.

Values

Knowing your values is a cornerstone of self-awareness. One of my colleagues shared a story with me recently about an experience she had with her son. He had come home after an evening at a teen coffee house. He was elated! He and his friend had found a large bag of silver dollars under a tree in the parking lot. They split the coins and her son was convinced that he could sell the silver dollars and get enough money to buy a new guitar. My colleague reported that, when she looked at the coins, some of them were in cases indicating they had been cared for. "Honey, this is somebody's collection," she told her son. "I'm not going to tell you what to do here, but I am going to ask you to think about what is the right thing to do." After thinking about it overnight, he decided to call the police and turn the coins in. She praised him profusely for "doing the right thing." By giving him the space to examine his values and praising him for making a good decision, Mom was reinforcing values of honesty, integrity, and concern for others. It is important as parents to look for teachable moments to instill values. When values are instilled early on, they become guiding principles that act as an inner compass, directing us through life. Our kids internalize rules for living that become almost an unconscious way of being. They are grounded in who they are and where they are going in life. In an age where our iGen kids are vulnerable to being negatively influenced by thousands of messages that bombard them every day from the internet, cell phones, and other forms of wireless technology, it is imperative that we are vigilant about teaching and instilling core values.

Strengths and Weaknesses

While values are learned and can be reinforced, we are all born with an inherent and unique set of personality traits. It is helpful to reflect on and determine areas of strength and areas of weakness. In chapter 2, I disclosed my struggles, not only with ADHD but also with a nonverbal learning disability which results in visual and spatial deficits. In other words, I have difficulties reading maps, getting from point A to point B, and organizing my physical space. I am aware that this is a major weakness for me. I have also learned that while I have struggles operating in the physical world, I am particularly adept at navigating in the world of what is unseen. For example, when I work with couples, I intuitively know how to "map out" the psychological landscape and assist them in moving from point A to point B in their relationship. This is a major strength for me. In coming to a point in life where I have identified and accepted my strengths and weaknesses, I am able to direct my energy where it most needs to be. I know when to ask for help and I know what kind of support I need. What is your greatest strength? What is your weakness? Can you talk about them without embarrassment or judgment?

If you want to teach your child to be self-aware, you have to first develop your own sense of self-awareness. In your daily routine with your child, how often do you identify and talk about feelings? Are you OK with anger? Are you OK with your child's anger? How tuned in are you to your physical states when feeling emotions? Do you know what your personal triggers are? How aware are you of your own self-defeating and default patterns of behavior? What are your values? What are your strengths and weaknesses? Take a look at the tips below. It may be useful for you to read through them and apply them to yourself before you begin working with your child.

Tips for Teaching Your Child Self-Awareness

- **Teach and instill feelings and feelings language:** There is no such thing as feeling "like" something. Feelings are generally described with one word: happy, mad, sad, relieved, etc. You can go on the internet and find examples of Feeling Charts that provide helpful pictures and descriptions of a variety of emotions.

- **Accept your feelings without judgment:** Feelings are neither bad nor good. They are messages that compel us to action and influence our decision making. For example, say you become aware that you are angry with your child for leaving a mess in the kitchen. You're not a bad parent for getting angry. Your anger is a signal that you have to do something, such as asking them to clean up and to respect the rules of the house.

- **Feelings are emotional states that take place in the body:** Revisit an intensely emotional experience your child had. Explore and identify the sensations involved in their body. Ask guiding questions such as, Where did you feel it in your body? Was your heart beating fast or slow? What was your breathing like? Were your palms sweating? Was your throat or other muscles tight? How did your stomach feel? Moving forward, guided questions such as these will help your child gain insight into how physical sensations are connected to emotional states.

- **Know your triggers:** Share the information above to teach your child what a trigger is. Review the examples and have your child identify the triggers that fit for them. Work with them to explore triggers that are unique to their experience.

- **Identify your self-defeating behaviors:** Review the information above on self-defeating behaviors with your child. Review the list to see if any of these are a fit. Work to identify any others that may not be mentioned above. Be open to sharing some of your own self-defeating behaviors to normalize this process for your child.

- **Identify your values**: A great way to identify and stay grounded in values is through affiliation with structured organizations such as church, boy and girl scouts, martial arts, sports, and meditation centers. Another powerful way to teach values to kids is by presenting ethical dilemmas. "What would you do if?" You can make a game of it or use it as a discussion topic over dinner. Have each family member take turns presenting an ethical dilemma and share beliefs.

- **Acknowledge and accept your strengths and weaknesses:** Help your child explore and identify their strengths and weaknesses. It is important to help them understand that we all have strengths and work areas. Talk to them about your strengths and weaknesses as a way to increase their comfort level in identifying their own.

Self-Management:

Self-management builds on the basis of self-awareness and is the ability to control our emotions so they don't control us. Think of it this way. Self-awareness is what *is* and self-management is what we *do* about what is. Again, I will return to the story of the young man who followed his impulse to jump off the roof of the garage. What would it have been like if, in that short window of time before he jumped, he took a breath and exhaled slowly? Remember our discussion about the "neuro" of emotional intelligence? Imagine him taking a breath, setting off a chain reaction of signals from the lower brain through the limbic system to the outer brain, and deciding to walk away. It can happen that fast. Taking a breath in a crucial moment is one example of using a self-management skill.

Emotional Regulation

Because our children's brains are not fully developed as teens, they need our support to learn how to regulate emotions. Emotions are like ocean waves. Some are calm and gentle, and some are fierce and crashing. Our task is to teach our teens to ride the waves without being pulled under. You have been doing this all along. Think back to when your child was a toddler. I'm sure you can remember a temper tantrum or two. Let's say you told your child, "No!" In response, they had an intense emotional experience. Maybe she threw herself on the floor and screamed at the top of her lungs. Maybe he stomped around and broke his toys. As a parent, you likely had a number of strategies up your sleeve to help your child calm down. Perhaps you diverted their attention by giving them a snack, or some sort of reassurance that everything was going to be OK. Some parents ignore their child's tantrums or provide time outs so as not to reinforce the behavior. Despite your attempts to communicate by use of language (What's wrong? Why don't you listen! Calm down!), you intuitively know that your toddler lacks the sophistication and skills to communicate their needs. As they move through childhood to adolescence and improve language skills, it is easy to get lulled into thinking that they have the capacity to articulate what they need. We become surprised as they seem to revisit the "terrible twos." We get tricked into believing that because they look mature, they are mature. We start to believe they don't need us to help them with emotional regulation, when, in fact, they need us more.

I had a mom in my office a few years ago. She was struggling immensely with her daughter, Amy, who had recently transitioned from a small private middle school to a large public high school. She didn't know anyone when she arrived and was stressed out about making friends and being accepted. Amy began to isolate in her room at home and snap at her mom when asked about her day. Her mother reported that she would "mope" around the house and bring everyone "down." She frequently locked herself in the bathroom and spent hours on her cell phone talking to friends from her old school. Amy became intensely emotional in my office with her mother in a session one day, stormed out, and slammed the door. As she was leaving, I told her it was OK to take a break, but we would really like her to come back. After several minutes Amy returned to my office and sullenly slumped down into a chair. I thanked her for coming back and asked her how she was feeling. She immediately started yelling at me. "How would you feel if your Mom was ragging on you all of the time?" Mom jumped in and yelled at her. "Be respectful!" I turned to mom and asked her to hold that thought while I worked with Amy to help her express her true feelings. I could feel the intensity in the room. I asked her to take a deep long breath with me. She rolled her eyes. I said, "come on, humor me." I began by demonstrating a deep long breath in through my nose and exhaled slowly through my mouth. She said, "why doesn't my mom have to do it?" I replied, "good point. Mom, how would you like to take a crack at this with us?" We took one breath together. I asked them to do it again. "One more time just for fun," I said. After three deep breaths, I noticed a shift in the energy. I asked her again how she was feeling and gave her some options from a feeling chart. "Really, really angry," she said. "Here is what I know about anger," I explained. "Anger is like a shield and there is usually another feeling behind it." She paused and began to sob in the chair. I gave her a few minutes and validated that it was not only OK to cry, but it was good for her. Amy expressed hurt and sadness for having to leave her school and not being able to see her friends. I helped her make a connection between her feelings of hurt and sadness, and angry acting out. I turned to Mom and asked her if she was aware of how much Amy was hurting. Mom had tears in her eyes. "No, I wasn't. I just thought she was mad and being selfish and disrespectful. I had no idea she was in this much pain." As Amy wept, her mother apologized for not understanding how stressed out she was over the transition to the new school. In future sessions when Amy got upset, rather than getting defensive and yelling, Mom became a more calm and nurturing presence. She became a better listener, learned to validate her daughter's feelings, and was much more open to respecting her point of view. Amy learned to identify and process feelings rather than acting out. As she became more adept at regulating her emotions in sessions, her mother was happy to report that Amy had been using these newfound skills at home and in school. Consider the tips below to help your teen regulate emotions.

- **Give them space:** When our kids are upset and in their lower brains (reptilian fight or flight), we are only adding fuel to the fire if we keep pushing them. Take a break and let them know you will revisit the topic later.

- **Understand that anger could be masking other emotions:** Don't always take anger at face value. Most often, when kids are presenting as angry, there is a more important underlying emotion they are struggling with.

- **Respect differing perspectives:** Sometimes we need to think about our children's point of view, (e.g., school life). Parents often forget about how important social life is to kids and only see through the lens of grades or performance. Remember, when kids are socially connected, they perform better in school and in life.

- **Bite your tongue:** Sometimes we have to take a breath and hold on to our thoughts. When you feel yourself getting worked up (breathing, heart rate, sweaty palms) and you are ready to blow, or you see your child is ready to blow, "bite your tongue" and wait for things to cool down.

- **Be calm:** Remember, feelings are contagious. Don't get pulled in. You may have to take a few deep breaths to center yourself before approaching your child. We have an energetic connection with our kids. The best way to help them regulate emotions is to approach with a calm presence. A calm presence is much more effective than words when our kids are struggling emotionally.

- **Validate feelings:** As I mentioned earlier, feelings aren't good or bad. Let your child know that whatever they are feeling is OK. When they calm down, encourage them to put words to their feelings.

- **Be a role model:** The better we are at regulating our emotions, the better our children will be. Talk about feelings with them and share techniques you use to regulate emotions and cope with stress (e.g., deep breathing, meditation, physical activity, reading, leisure activities).

- **Consider therapy:** If your child struggles with regulating emotions despite your best efforts, consider seeing a therapist for help. There may be a deep underlying issue that needs to be addressed professionally.

Impulse Control

Think back to your first few months away from home on a college campus with a bunch of high energy kids your age. So much newfound freedom and so many choices to make! The *Annual Review of Clinical Psychology* is a widely established clinical journal that publishes research articles. In January 2019, it was reported that children with high self-control perform better academically. A very important aspect of self-control is the capacity to manage impulses. Impulse control is the ability to delay gratification and stay focused on long-term goals, such as getting good grades and accepted into good colleges. According to the review, nearly all students struggle with conflicts between long term academic goals and short-term non-academic goals that they find more alluring and gratifying in the moment. Lack of impulse control can lead to self-defeating behaviors that compromise academic performance. Last year, I interviewed 50 college students who corroborated this evidence. It was no surprise that cell phones, social media and video games were major distractors to focusing on school work. The video game "Fortnite" was identified as a significant problem on college campuses. Lack of impulse control can lead to other self-defeating behaviors, such as skipping classes, substance abuse, bullying, and procrastination. Parents, now is the time to work with your child on learning to manage impulses and avoid self-defeating behaviors. Take a look at the tips below.

- **Get clear on the big picture:** The more grounded your child is in "big picture" goals, the more capacity they will have to manage impulses and avoid self-defeating behaviors. Talk about big picture goals (e.g., GPAs, areas of study, career goals). Let them know how excited you are for them. Have a "SWOT" discussion in which you identify Strengths, Weaknesses, Opportunities, and Threats. What is your greatest strength? What is a work area for you? What are your opportunities? What are possible threats to your big picture goals moving forward in school? Write these down in a journal for future reference.

- **Establish clear expectations and boundaries:** Establish clear expectations and boundaries around school attendance, study time, substance use, screen time, time with friends, and curfews. Stress that your expectations are not about controlling but instead for success in school. Clear expectations and boundaries will raise your child's level of awareness, resulting in better impulse control and fewer self-defeating behaviors.

- **Self-Monitoring:** When your child engages in a self-defeating behavior, stay calm and help them think through the incident. Ask them some questions. Where were you? What was happening? Can you remember how you were feeling? What were you thinking? Work to help them identify a choice they can use next time that will result in a better outcome.

- **Teach your teen to delay gratification:** Let them know that they can go out with friends when they finish their homework. Encourage them to stay away from phones and social media while they are doing school work. Set aside time for them to enjoy electronics as a reward. Have them turn off cell phones before they go to bed or move them into a different room.

- **Encourage your child to breathe:** Teen years are full of excitement and emotion which creates challenges with impulse control. Taking time to breathe calms the brain down, resulting in higher levels of self-awareness and better decision making. Coach your child to remember to breathe in the heat of the moment before making decisions that could result in self-defeating behavior.

Social Skills

To this point, I have been discussing emotional intelligence within the context of self-awareness (i.e., being aware of emotions in any given moment) and self-management (i.e., how we manage our emotions). Following his book on emotional intelligence in 1995, Dr. Goleman wrote another very important book in 2006: *Social Intelligence: The Revolutionary New Science of Human Relation-*

ships. In his book, Dr. Goleman introduces two areas important in the development of social skills: *social awareness* and *social facility.* You can think about these in much the same way I discussed self-awareness and self-management above. Social awareness is your child's ability to sense how others are thinking and feeling. Social facility is your child's ability to interact most effectively based on this knowledge. Social awareness is what *is* and social facility is what we *do* about what is. In his book, Dr. Goleman celebrates the emergence of "social neuroscience" and its contributions to our understanding of how we relate and interact with each other as human beings. As previously discussed, we now know about mirror neurons. Goleman describes them like an internal "wi-fi" system. Our brains synchronize with each other on a primal level, allowing us to make quick decisions on how to interact socially. He underscores the importance of brain plasticity. By practicing social skills, we build and strengthen pathways in our brains responsible for successful execution. Socially intelligent teens are able to connect well with others and have their needs met in social situations.

Social Awareness

At the core of social awareness is the ability to sense how others are thinking and feeling. We do this by reading and interpreting both verbal and nonverbal cues. Verbal cues are generally communicated through spoken language. Nonverbal cues involve body posture, body movement, facial expressions, voice tones, and pace of speech. As we become aware of these cues, we need to put them in context with the social setting we are in. What may be appropriate at a high school pep fest would not be appropriate in the library.

I learned about the importance of social awareness in my first job out of high school working as a waiter in a busy restaurant. Being socially aware could mean the difference between walking home with a nice wad of cash in your pocket or being frustrated by how low your tips were. As I approached my tables, I learned to read facial expressions and body language within seconds and adapt to the needs of my customers. A group of businessmen coming in for lunch dressed in suits with serious facial expressions, monotone voices, and rigid body postures are not concerned about small talk with me. They are focused on each other, talking about work, and in a hurry to eat lunch and get back to the office. They want quick, efficient service, and nothing else. Sitting in a booth next to my businessmen are two women who come in from the bar with a martini in hand. I notice that they are chatting and laughing with a relaxed body posture. They smile warmly and begin to engage me in conversation. I quickly assess that they are not in a hurry and want to enjoy themselves. Part of the experience for them is to chat and share some humor with me. I take time out to smile, laugh, and joke with them. At the table next to them, a mom and dad sit with an infant and a toddler, who is a bundle of energy. I observe Mom's red face and watch as Dad reaches over the table, trying get his kid to sit still. It appears as if they have been out shopping all day and are needing to feed their kids. I sense that they are both tired and worried about their kids making a scene in the restaurant. I bring crayons and crackers to the table for the kids, and Mom thanks me profusely. They vent with me about their busy day and I tell

them they have nothing to worry about with the kids. "I understand, I was a kid once myself."

Social Facility

Social facility is the action phase of social skills. We have
received and interpreted information and are now responding. If
we receive information verbally and nonverbally, it makes sense
that our response is both verbal and nonverbal. Some important
components of social facility are attending to the energy, self-presentation, anticipating needs, active listening, demonstrating
concern, and shaping the outcome. Below are examples of how I
used these skills to interact with my customers.

Attending to the energy: In the restaurant, as I approached my
table of businessmen, I matched their energy by being busi-
ness-like, serious, and efficient. As I approached my table with
the women drinking martinis, I used humor, a more relaxed pace,
and small talk.

Self-Presentation: With the businessmen, I presented myself as a
confident, no nonsense professional. I shared my casual, person-
able side with the women sitting in the booth.

Anticipating Needs: When the young family came in, I quickly
assessed and anticipated that a diversion was needed to avoid a
meltdown. I brought crackers and coloring crayons to the table.

Active Listening: With my businessmen, I demonstrated active
listening by repeating their orders word for word to make sure I
got it right. I was really busy the day the two women came into
my section. I had ten other tables in various stages of their dining
experience. In order to connect with them and listen actively, I

had to put all of my anxious thoughts to the side (e.g., check to table six, milk with meal to table one, I'm tired, I can't wait to get off of my shift, my feet are killing me). I focused my attention one hundred percent on them. They spoke with me about a trip they had been on with their families together in Mexico. I shared a funny story about a fishing trip I went on while I was there.

Demonstrating Concern: I could tell that my young family, with the high energy kids, were very flustered when they came into my section. I had a caring expression on my face and I spoke softly, assuring them that they didn't have to worry about their kids making a scene.

Shaping the Outcome: In each scenario, my goals were the same. I wanted my patrons to have a good time and I wanted to get a good tip. I had to be socially aware and adjust my responses to optimize the outcome for all of us.

As Baby Boomer and GenX parents, we grew up in a very different environment than our kids. Think back to the old neighborhoods. We got up every day and played all kinds of sports and games with each other: kick the can, capture the flag, pom-pom poll away, football, baseball, and the like. We had opportunities every day, all day, to learn and practice social skills, and it happened naturally; we didn't even realize that we were learning anything—we were just having fun. Think about all of the arguments you had as kids playing games. We would often get into such heated disagreements that the game would stop and we would have to negotiate, make compromises, and change rules for the benefit of the group. We also had to tend to each other's emotions, like sticking up for someone who was feeling hurt or being taken advantage of. Sometimes, physical boundaries would be violated and we would have to make rules about being respect-ful within the context of a physical activity in which we were competing. We were "synchronized" with each other. At home, we spent much more time with our parents, observing them interact at the grocery store, in church, and with strangers. We learned about humor, sarcasm, and all of the subtleties of implicit and explicit social communication.

Our iGen kids are experiencing a serious deprivation of basic human contact critical for healthy social and emotional development. In his book, Dr. Goleman reported findings from a 2004 survey of 4,830 participants on the impact of television and internet use in the United States. In doing the math, they concluded that for every hour on the internet, face to face contact with friends, coworkers, and family fell by 24 minutes. Let's put this into perspective. In 2004, it was estimated that the average person in America spent 3 hours and 39 minutes per day watching television or on the internet. In chapter 6, I referred to informa-tion from the Pew Research Center indicating that cell phone ownership crossed the 50 percent threshold late in 2012, right when teen depression and suicide began to rise. By 2015, 73 percent of teens had access to smartphones. It is estimated that our iGen kids are spending a minimum of 6 hours per day on some form of electronic device. Imagine how this translates to lost opportuni-ties to develop social and emotional intelligence! Below is a list of seven skills that I believe are particularly important to focus on as you move forward with your child.

- **Active listening:** This is the art of conversation. Active listeners refrain from interrupting, waiting their turn to speak. They maintain eye contact and use body language to communicate interest. In conversation, an active listener asks questions to gain clarity and paraphrases, or repeats back information to ensure that they have a mutual understanding.

- **Attunement:** Attunement is being fully present for another person. It is the ability to put all thoughts about yourself aside and pay complete attention. You "tune in" to body language, facial expressions, and voice tones. Your verbal and nonverbal responses indicate genuine care and concern. Kids can sense immediately when a parent or caregiver is distracted or disingenuous.

- **Boundaries:** Personal boundaries are guidelines, rules or limits that a person creates to identify reasonable, safe, and permissible ways for other people to behave towards them. It is imperative that kids learn how to set physical and psychological boundaries for themselves. Examples of physical boundaries are: physical space (e.g., how close you can sit or stand next to me); touch (e.g., how, when, and where you can touch me); personal space (e.g., room, house, yard); and belongings. Examples of psychological boundaries are: personal feelings, beliefs, and values (e.g., my feelings, beliefs, and values are OK. I get to decide where and with whom to share them).

- **Assertiveness:** An assertive student asks for what they want and need in a respectful and open manner. They use "I" statements; "When you don't post my grade after I finish an assignment, I feel anxious because I lose track of how I am doing in class. If you are unable to post grades immediately, is there another way that we could communicate so I know where I stand?"

- **Refusal skills:** Refusal skills build on assertiveness and are crucial for kids to practice in order to avoid self-defeating behaviors, such as smoking, substance abuse, skipping school, and hanging out with kids who get in trouble. Saying no sounds easy, however, it can result in a tremendous amount of peer pressure. The more kids practice saying no, the more comfortable they become over time.

- **Conflict resolution:** An important aspect of growing up is learning how to address conflicts. Your child needs to communicate their side of the story clearly (without yelling and screaming) and be open to listening to the other's point of view. Once this has been established, both parties engage in negotiations to explore options to resolve the conflict. The end goal is to reach a compromise that works for both parties.

- **Social responsibility:** In order to function productively in the world, it is vital for us to understand that we are part of something bigger than ourselves. Our actions, good or bad, have a ripple effect that touches family, friends, and the broader community.

Empathy

I learned about empathy from my parents early on in life. We used to get calls from bill collectors looking for payments on utilities. I answered the phone one day and a person from the gas company asked if my parents were available. I responded with a "no" and he began to talk very sternly with me. "Tell your parents that if they don't pay the gas bill, we're going to shut it off!" I remember talking to my parents about it and being very concerned. I could see the stress in their faces as I relayed the message from the "angry man" on the phone. As much as we struggled financially, my parents always held firm to their values of service to others. They were frequently involved in projects helping people in need. I remember confronting them one day after I learned they gave money to a woman who was in danger of losing her apartment. I was mad. "Why are you giving someone three hundred dollars when we can't pay the gas bill!? My father looked at me and said, "because she needs it more than we do." He explained that the woman had young children who needed food and a place to live. If they got evicted, they could be separated from each other. These were not uncommon experiences in my family. My parents had enormous empathy and compassion for people. My mother, in her early forties, after raising a family of nine children, started a non-profit agency whose mission is to help families "overcome barriers, believe in themselves, and soar to new heights." She started by putting a large basket out in church, encouraging people to contribute food items to help those less fortunate. Forty-plus years later, Interfaith Outreach is a multi-million-dollar organization not only involved in providing food, but clothing, employment assistance, affordable housing, childcare, after school programs, and a myriad of other social services.

Empathy builds on all of the other EQ skills discussed thus far. Research shows that students high in empathy are more engaged in classrooms, have better communication skills, and higher academic achievement. Parents, research aside; if you only get one take away from this book (and I hope you get many), empathy is what your child (and our world) needs most! We tend to think of empathy as the ability to understand the experience of others. While this is generally true, it is actually more complex. Dr. Goleman defines empathy on three levels. The first level, *cognitive empathy*, refers to our intellectual understanding of how others think. The second level, *emotional empathy*, is how we pick up on the emotions of others. Level three, *empathic concern*, goes beyond thoughts and feelings, to taking action. My parents understood, on an intellectual level, that the woman with the kids was thinking, "I don't know what to do! What's going to happen with my kids?" On an emotional level, they connected with her frustration, fear, and deep love for her children. Based on their understanding of her situation and emotional state, my parents were motivated to take action and do something to help.

I am grateful to my parents for modeling and teaching me how to have empathy for others. I not only observed but also had multiple opportunities to practice empathy throughout my childhood. One of my earliest memories was being down in our basement with my mother and gang of siblings making decoupages for a school fundraiser. We laughed and had fun as we applied cutouts onto stained pieces of wood with a fresh coating of lacquer to finish our masterpieces. "Mom, are people actually going to buy these? Why are we doing this?" "The money we raise will help people living in poverty in Biafra," she explained. The following day at school, we watched a documentary reporting on the impact of living in poverty in Biafra. Some of it was really hard to watch.

The fact that I still remember it today, like yesterday, tells me it was a great way to learn how to have empathy for others.

As you can see by Goleman's layered definition above, learning true empathy is complex. It takes practice and exposure. How then, are our iGen kids, who are so intensely wired into electronics, going to have time to learn and practice empathy? In 2018, Common Sense Media reported that teenagers (13-18 yrs.) spend about nine hours daily online. Tweens (8-12 yrs.) spend 6 hours online, while kids (0-8) spend about 50 minutes. Results from a study by the University of Michigan found a 40 percent decrease in college students' empathy levels over the past 30 years. The sharpest drop occurred in 2000 when digital technology gained in popularity among college students. Lack of empathy in teens contributes to teasing, bullying, and cheating on tests. As parents, it is important for us to model and teach our kids not only to understand how others are thinking and feeling, but also to take action out of empathic concern. In a 2018 article about social and emotional learning, Michelle Barba identified several competencies for teachers to teach empathy to students. Below are some of her tips for teachers that I have modified for you (parents) to use with your child.

- **Foster Emotional Literacy:** An emotionally literate child is able to read and accurately interpret the emotions of others. Parents prioritize face-to-face contact and talk about feelings regularly in your household and day to day activities (e.g., dinner table) to enhance your child's abilities.

- **Self-regulation:** Provide opportunities for practices that help manage mood, such as meditation, yoga, deep breathing, quiet time without electronic devices, soft music, body movement, and other forms of physical activity. Self-regulation allows kids to keep emotions in check, giving them more capacity to have empathy for others.

- **Perspective Taking:** This is the act of emotionally and psychologically stepping into another's shoes. Have discussions with your kids about taking perspectives of others (e.g., kids with disabilities, kids that get bullied, and kids from low-income families who can't keep up with the latest styles). Consider activities you can engage in together as a family to gain a deeper understanding of another's perspective (e.g., fasting for a day to understand hunger or participating in an overnight sleep out to learn more about homelessness).

- **Moral Imagination:** Books and emotionally-charged films can prompt empathetic feelings. For example, "Because of Winn-Dixie" is both a book and a movie about a motherless young girl who moves to a new town and struggles to make friends until she comes across a loveable stray dog. There are hundreds of books and movies that demonstrate empathy through a variety of characters and storylines. Brainstorm a list of these with friends or other parents and set aside time for reading together as a family or a regular movie night.

- **Moral Identity:** We can help our kids develop moral identities by coming up with mantras, slogans, or family mottos. Growing up, my family motto was to live by the golden rule; treat others the way you would like to be treated. Take some time and have a family discussion about your shared values and come up with a slogan of your own. Check in periodically to assess how well you are following your motto.

- **Practicing acts of kindness:** Kindness is always good and benefits both parties. Being kind is what helps children tune in to others' feelings and needs. As we have discussed, tuning into feelings and understanding needs is a big part of learning empathy. The more opportunities we give our children to practice acts of kindness, the more "we" and less "me" oriented they become.

- **Collaboration:** Empathy is not a selfish act. It takes place within relationships. When our kids team up with others for a cause they are passionate about, they realize their participation is about being part of something bigger than themselves. Cooperative work fosters empathy skills of encouraging others, disagreeing respectfully, and resolving conflicts.

- **Moral Courage:** Teach your children about moral courage! The best way for me to explain this to you is to tell a personal story. When I was nine years old, we used to have very competitive spelling and math contests in my classroom. The teacher would start the clock and we would all begin doing our problems. When we were finished, we would have to stand up from our seat. The students who finished last were often chastised. In particular, there were two kids (brothers) in the class who always finished last. The teacher encouraged us to make demeaning group chants to them for finishing last. I was very troubled by this. One day, I finally told my father about what was going on in the classroom. He said, "David, that's wrong. You have to speak out for these kids." A few weeks later, we were in class and as we all stood up, finished with our math problems, the teacher lead the class in a chant directed at the two brothers: "Dumb bunny, Dumb bunny, Dumb bunny!" I couldn't take it anymore. I was so afraid of her that I was shaking. I heard my dad's voice telling me that this was wrong. I spoke up and told her to stop. "You can't do that! That's wrong!" The entire class went silent for about a minute. The silence ended with many of my friends in the classroom verbally agreeing with what I said. I was kicked out of class for having a "frenzy." I cried when I got home because I thought I would get in trouble. Instead, my father praised me for "doing the right thing." My children love this story. Parents, I am sure you have stories about moral courage. Share these stories with your kids as a way to teach them to embrace and practice acts of moral courage.

- **Grow Change-Makers:** If we provide our kids with opportunities to help others, we not only activate empathy in them, but strengthen their identities as change-makers. For example, Feed My Starving Children is a non-profit agency that uses volunteers to package nutritious meals for children all over the world. They host a number of different groups, from Cub Scouts, to church youth groups, to kids who choose this activity as part of their birthday party. When they finish, they learn how many meals were made and how many people they served. In this way, it becomes personal and helps them to learn, first-hand, about the impact they can have on the world as change-makers.

Empathy Exercise: Volunteer with your child for a good cause somewhere in your community.

Chapter 10:
Step 7—Set Realistic Goals and Coach Your Child to Success

As your child's parent/coach, the best way you can help them achieve goals is by building confidence. Psychologist Albert Bandura, in the 1970s, developed what has been widely accepted as an effective model for instilling confidence, known as "self-efficacy theories." Self-efficacy is a person's belief in their ability to succeed in a goal-directed activity, such as getting good grades and getting accepted into a good college. The stronger your child's belief in their ability to get good grades and get into a good college, the more active they become in pursuit of the goal. And the more active they become, the more successful they will be. Before you help your child with goal setting, I want to introduce you to Dr. Bandura's sources of self-efficacy. I will refer to these later.

- *Prior accomplishments:* When we are lacking confidence and experiencing self-doubt, it is helpful to reflect on mastery experiences. Mastery experiences are past performance accomplishments. Think about your child. What are some significant accomplishments they have achieved in the past? Helping your child reflect on past successes is the most dependable source of confidence-building information because it is based on personal experience.

- *Vicarious learning from role models:* One of the best ways to learn is through others who have been successful at the goal you are trying to achieve. Think of vicarious learning as a process of observing, learning, imitating, and acting. Who can you think of that would be a good role model for your child to interact with to learn how to perform well at getting good grades and getting accepted into a good college? An ideal situation is to connect your child with a student a year or two older.

- *Verbal Persuasion:* When setting goals with your child, be positive and let them know you believe in their ability to succeed. As parents, we know our children's character strengths more than anyone else. Speaking out loud and celebrating them is very motivational! Be authentic. Give them honest, constructive, positive feedback. Challenge negative self-talk and replace it with positive affirmations.

- *Arousal/managing emotions:* We all experience anxiety when we are trying something new. Work with your child on establishing anxiety-reducing practices. Deep breathing and meditation are the absolute number one way to achieve calm. Yoga is a great stress-reducer and has become more and more popular with teens and young adults. Encourage your child to incorporate physical activity into daily routines. We now are aware, through the field of neuroscience, that a great deal of stress gets stored in our bodies. Physical activity calms the body, which calms the mind. The calmer your child is, the more brainpower they have. Often, when we get anxious, we develop negative self-talk about our ability to succeed at a goal. In the field of psychology, we call these "distorted" thoughts. Most of us have had them at one time or another when under stress. Coach your child through dialogue to challenge the reality of negative self-talk and move towards positivity.

- *Imaginary experiences*: Imaginary experiences help your child visualize success. Visualizing success will strengthen the neurological pathways in your child's brain that are responsible for performing well in school. It's like mental practice. Athletes use this for performance in sports. A major league pitcher may take time before the game and imagine every situation he will be up against and picture himself being successful. When it is game time, he will be much better prepared.

There are some critical parts of goal setting you need to be aware of when working with your child to be successful. Goals need to be specific, measurable, achievable, and time-limited, and it is very important to write them down. Writing goals down legitimizes your work together. Below is an example of using confidence building coaching techniques to help a young woman successfully complete her first ever marathon. As you read through, think of how you can use these same coaching techniques to help your child get good grades.

Step 1: Identify the goal and write it down

In my first meeting with this young woman, I ask her, "What is your goal?" She tells me her goal is to complete her first-ever marathon. "Do you want to train to finish, or are you going for a particular time frame?" She explains that her main goal is to finish but it would be really cool if she could make it in under five hours.

"Ok, write that down in your journal." The fact that this is her first-ever marathon, I ask her for a six-month time commitment. She agrees.

Step 2: List the tasks needed to obtain the goal

Because she is a novice to long-distance running, I tell her where she can buy a good pair of shoes and running apparel appropriate for weather conditions. She needs a water bottle and a stopwatch so she can keep track of time. I strongly suggest she gets a heart rate monitor. I work with her to establish a target heart rate to stay in while she is running to keep safe and give her dietary information about carbohydrates, protein, and fats as related to long-distance training. I make sure she knows what complex carbohydrates are. We meet to map out the training schedule. For the first three weeks, she will walk and run 15 miles per week. From there, mileage and frequency will be added incrementally as she can handle it.

Step 3: Start working on the tasks

We have a check in the first week to see if she was able to get the right equipment. I ask her if she has stocked her house with foods that will give her energy. On our third weekly check-in, she tells me that she is getting a shin splint. I instruct her to reduce her mileage and ice it after she runs.

Step 4: Add to the tasks as needed

I continue to monitor her progress. She is in week six, running 20 miles per week, pain-free. I add more miles to her weekly regimen and recommend adding more complex carbohydrates to her diet. She works her way up to 70 miles per week in her final month of training. I instruct her to taper down to 45-50 miles a week for the next few weeks to give her body a chance to fully recover before the big day.

Step 5: Check off the tasks as they are completed

In our weekly meetings, we check off tasks that have been completed. Each time she finishes a task, we talk about it. We review the steps she took to accomplish the task and how she overcame obstacles or setbacks along the way. I praise her for her hard work.

Step 6: When all of the tasks are complete, determine if the goal has been met

In the final week, she runs 20 miles and takes two days of rest before the marathon. She finishes the run in 4 hours and 55 minutes without injury. We celebrate her accomplishments. She proudly sports her marathon medal around her neck and reports that she can't wait to wear her "finisher" tee-shirt to Thanksgiving dinner with the family.

Throughout our coaching process, I utilize Bandura's sources of self-efficacy to instill confidence and increase motivation. "What is the most challenging feat you have ever accomplished," I ask her. She says, "I have never been a big runner or athlete, so I don't know how to answer that question." "It doesn't have to be something athletic," I explain. "I was in the school musical my junior year," she says. I use this *prior accomplishment* to help her connect emotionally with a past experience of success and she tells me it was a major commitment. "I had to practice every day for three months!" In order to keep up with her school work and remain in the musical, she had to give up screen time and social media at night. "I had to get up early on the weekends to practice!" That was really hard because I like to sleep on the weekends." "Tell me about opening night," I ask. "I was so scared before I went on stage that I thought I was gonna throw up!" She describes how she "channeled" her nervous energy into her performance and "nailed" every line. I watch her as she remembers this experience. Her eyes widen and she begins to smile. "At the end of the play, we received a standing ovation and I was presented with a bouquet of roses from my parents. It was the most exhilarating thing that ever happened to me!"

She is really excited and fired up as she speaks to me. I seize this opportunity to engage her in an *imaginary experience* about her marathon goal. "Let's imagine you are at the start of the marathon. You have been practicing, making sacrifices, getting up early, and you are ready to go. You feel nervous, but you channel all of that energy into your performance. See yourself running and 'nailing' it, mile after mile. At the finish line is a crowd of people giving you a standing ovation. You feel exhilarated as you cross the finish line!"

As we continue our discussion, I have her imagine barriers or road blocks she might experience along the way. "When I get anxious, I start to doubt myself, and sometimes find myself on the couch with a pint of ice cream and a bag of cookies, binging on Netflix," she says. I work to help her *manage emotions.* "What about the marathon makes you most anxious?" "I feel like an imposter out there with all of those skinny athletic people!" "How do you think they felt before their first marathon?" "They were probably a little scared themselves," she says. "When a person is trying to learn something new, are they an imposter, or are they simply someone who is trying to learn something new?" "Yeah, I know what you mean," she replies. "Have you ever been to a marathon and watched runners cross the finish line?" "Yes, I have," she says. "It was really cool." "Was everyone who crossed the finish line skinny?" "No," she responds. "I was surprised at how many different body types crossed the line." "Was everybody running across the finish line?" "No, some people were walking." "Were the people who ran across the finish line happier than the ones who didn't?" "Actually, no", she says. She explains that the runners who walked across were just as happy, "if not happier." From here, we make a plan for the next time she is feeling anxious and finds herself headed for the couch. I instruct her to take some time alone to do some deep breathing and get herself grounded in her goal and her motivation. As she meditates, she reflects: "This is a challenge that I have always wanted to do for myself. It is not about how fast. I don't have to be better than everyone else and I don't have to be skinny. If I have to walk for parts of the run, it is OK. After all, this is my first one. I can think of my training in the same way. I don't have to be perfect, but I do have to be consistent with my workouts. If I am having a day where I am not feeling super motivated, I can shorten my work out, but I need to be committed to staying off of the couch and put some effort in."

As a coach, and having been coached, I am aware of how impactful it is to learn from someone you admire and feel you can relate to. I introduce her to a client I coached a few years ago who ran her first marathon in 5 hours and 10 minutes. She is now on her fourth marathon and recently ran one in 4 hours and 30 minutes. Working with mentors is a great opportunity for *vicarious learning*. My former client meets with her and shares strategies she has learned to be successful. She agrees to do some training runs with her and give her feedback on how she can improve. She introduces her to a running group she has been in at her local club. My client joins the group and later reflects on how she became a "much better runner" by having support from "people who have been there." I often talk to my clients about this kind of learning as "feeling it in your bones." As I have learned more about neuroscience, I have become aware that feeling it in your bones is not so far from the truth!

In month four of her training, she mentions that she feels tired, as if she wants to quit. "This is really time-consuming! I don't know about this. I'm not sure if I have what it takes!" I engage her in a *verbal persuasion* dialogue. "Remember back when you told me the story about getting a part in the high school play and 'nailing' the lines? Do you remember all of the sacrifices you had to make: giving up electronics at night, waking up earlier on the weekends, and practicing your lines every day for three months?" "I sure do," she replies. "Do you remember taking a bow at the end of the performance?" "I will never forget it." "Can you see yourself taking a bow at the finish line of the marathon?" "That would be so cool," she exclaims! I reflect on my experience with her for the past four months. "I know you can do this! I admire your commitment and your courage to challenge yourself by facing your fears and doing something you have never done! You are hard-working and tenacious! It has been an honor to witness this with you and watch you getting stronger every day! You've got this!"

In the story above I use a sports metaphor to illustrate confidence building coaching techniques. Below is an example of a structure for you to consider to set academic goals for your child. As you look at it, think of how you can use *prior accomplishments, imaginary experiences, managing emotions, vicarious learning,* and *verbal persuasion* to coach your child to success in school.

Step 1: Identify a goal and write it down

Teen:

- Achieve a 3.5 grade point average.

Parent:

- Based on your knowledge of your child's ability and how they're functioning academically, assess whether or not this is a realistic goal.

Step 2: List tasks needed to obtain the goal

Teen:

- I will maintain 90 percent attendance.
- If an absence occurs, I will commit to getting the information I missed from a peer or my teacher.
- I will commit to using my instructor's office hours if I need support. Office hours are Wednesdays and Fridays from 3:30 to 5:30 pm.
- I will commit to refraining from using social media while I am studying.
- I will spend two hours a week studying for each one of my classes.

- I will commit to waking up no later than 11:00 am on weekends to study.
- I will check in with my parents once per week to update my progress.

Parent:

- I will check in with my child every week to see how they're doing.
- I will create a structure of support and accountability for them to succeed.

Step 3: Start working on the tasks

Teen:

- I will begin working on these tasks at the beginning of fall semester on September 4th

Parent:

- I will commit to monitoring my child's progress.

Step 4: Add to tasks as needed

Teen:

- If I discover that something else is needed, I will add it to my task list.

Parent:

- I will continue to monitor progress, provide encouragement, and assist my child to add tasks to their list if/ when needed.

Step 5: Check off the tasks as they are completed

Teen:

- I will keep a record of my tasks and check them off as I complete them.

Parent:

- Each time your teen finishes a goal, talk about it.
- Praise them for their efforts.
- Review steps she/he took to accomplish it.
- If there were obstacles experienced along the way, discuss what was done to overcome them.

Step 6: When all of the tasks are complete, determine if the goal has been met.

Teen:

- At the end of the semester, I will evaluate my progress.

Parent:

- When your child comes toward the end of a goal period, reflect on progress and make sure to provide constructive feedback.
- Talk about what went well and where there is room for improvement.
- Acknowledge your child's hard work!

Chapter 10 Exercise: Have a meeting with your child and orient them to this goal-setting process. As you guide your child through academic goals, use the coaching techniques from the marathon example above to keep them motivated and on track.

Chapter 11:
Step 8—Putting it all Together

We have come a long way to get to this final step. You have not only gained insight into your child, yourself, and the unique struggles our iGen kids are facing, but have developed skills to promote mental fitness. It is now time to put it all together. In the paragraphs below, I will discuss how you can assist your child in laying the groundwork and covering all of the bases necessary for applying to get into colleges.

Empower and Respect

It happens so fast! Your child is blossoming into a young adult right in front of your eyes. Think about all of the skills they have learned and integrated throughout this process. It's time to empower and respect them as major players in their college journey. Easier said than done! I get parents in my office all of the time who love their kids so much that they want to control every aspect of their life. I worked with a dad who was a very high-powered businessman with a "type (triple) A" personality. I engaged him and his son in a dialogue about college. Dad took over the conversation and quickly turned it into a lecture about where his son should volunteer, when he should begin applying to colleges, and what classes he needed to take once he got there. The young man shrunk in the chair and shut down. I encouraged Dad to slow down and listen. "Dad, I have already found a service project that I think would be good to put on a college application," he said. I worked to educate Dad to show him that, in spite of all of his passion, he had inadvertently disrespected and disempowered his child. I stressed the importance of including his child not only in the discussion, but also in the process moving forward. In our zeal to help our kids we sometimes forget that the focus needs to be on what is best for them; not best for us.

Help Your Child Take Ownership

As Dad backed off, his son began to take more responsibility for his college application process. He wanted to volunteer in an after-school program helping high needs kids work on writing skills. He loved to write himself, and was thinking about getting into a journalism program in college. "I would have a chance to help kids in need and have something on my college application that could help for journalism school," he said. I praised him for using his critical thinking skills. I also complemented Dad for doing such a good job of instilling values in his son. As Dad's perspective began to shift out of himself, his son sat upright in the chair, perked up, and began to really take ownership. "I'm going to talk to Mr. Thompson. He's an English teacher who is in charge of the school newspaper. He studied journalism in college. Maybe he can give me some ideas to help me with my application." Our budding young adults need our help, however, as parents, we need to find a balance between offering support and empowering them to take ownership.

Preparing for the SAT and ACT

Many teens report that SAT and ACT exams are the toughest part of the college application experience. Have a discussion about the importance of test preparation. Study guides and practice tests are available online. Your child may want to try taking both the SAT and ACT. Most colleges will accept either. The test with the highest score may help with admission. In an article from October 8th, 2019, *The Minneapolis Star and Tribune* reported that, starting in September of 2020, students will be able to retake **parts** of the ACT exam up to 12 times. No longer will there be a requirement to take the entire exam over to improve scores. Some people hire private tutors to help prepare for the exams. Regardless of strategy, it is important to help reduce your child's anxiety. SAT and ACT scores are important factors in getting into a college, but not everything. Each college has a different set of admission requirements. Make sure you become familiar with the requirements of the colleges your child is interested in.

Timing is Everything

Many of us dream about college for our kids from the moment they are born. We start educational IRAs and buy savings bonds. We begin planting seeds early on about the importance of getting a college education. Well-meaning as we are, we can go overboard. Starting the process too soon can be a waste of our time and create anxiety for our kids. There is a really helpful tool from "College On Line Prep" that breaks down college prep tasks beginning in your teen's junior year. Check out this link that provides an easy to follow visual timeline:

http://static.squarespace.com/static/527cc9ffe4b-06105448def23/t/5390d40ee4b021878060633e/1402000398123/CEG-College-Prep.pdf

I suggest you print this out and keep it on your refrigerator.

Get Clear About Finances

I have very recently put two of my three children through college and my third is working on his degree as we speak. When my oldest daughter was a junior in high school, my wife and I had to sit down to get clear about financing college. We had to look at our budget (thank God she's an MBA and smart as a whip about these things!) and determine where and how we could "tighten the family belt." We researched and learned about the FAFSA—a creature that didn't exist when we went to college. And we looked at a variety of student and parent loan options. Lisa Heffernan is the founder of a website for parents called *Grown and Flown* (grownandflown.com). She provides thorough information about the nuts and bolts of paying for college. We found her information very useful in our process.

You Don't Have to Do This Alone

It is easy to feel overwhelmed by all of the details around the college application experience. It's OK to ask for help. A great place to start is with your child's academic counselor in high school. Make sure you prepare a list of questions before meeting. School counselors generally have the most up-to-date information about applying for colleges. Look for classes in your community education catalog. These forums provide opportunities for you to meet other parents to gain support and share ideas. If you feel you need more, you can hire a parenting consultant or a coach for guidance.

Getting Into a Good College May Not Be as Hard as You Think

We tend to think of good colleges as institutions like Yale, Harvard, Princeton, Stanford, and other elite schools. I would argue that a good college is one that is a "total" fit for your child. In chapter 3, I introduced a popular framework from the field of counseling and psychology to assess mental fitness; a "bio/psycho/social" model. To reiterate, this means that, to succeed in school, your child needs to be physically healthy, psychologically sound, and socially connected. It is easy to get swayed into thinking that the best thing we can do for our kids is to get them into the most prestigious learning environment possible. This can be a set up for disappointment. Your child may not get accepted, or if they do, it might not be the right fit for them.

Dylan and his parents came to see me for coaching when he was 18-years old, a freshman in college, and had recently been placed on academic probation. Dylan had been a straight "A" student through high school with an affinity for math and science. His parents met 20 years ago at an elite private college. As they reflected on the experience, they described their college days as romantic, challenging, and exhilarating times. It had been a dream of theirs, from the time that Dylan was born, that he attend their college Alma Mater. Dylan shared the dream and very much wanted to be a part of his parent's legacy. Dad looked bewildered in our first meeting. "I don't understand, it was a snap for him to get accepted. He had perfect grades in high school and scored very high on his ACT and SAT. How can someone so smart fail so many classes?" "I think I need to talk to the Dean of the school," Mom said. "There must be something wrong with how they are teaching when such a good student gets bad grades like that." I turned to Dylan, "What do think about all of this?" "I have been racking my brain. It wasn't that the classes were all that hard. And the professors seemed OK, they just didn't have time to talk to anyone. The worst part was the kids at my school. They were really snobby and I didn't feel like I could relate to them. They were so phony and superficial. All they care about is what they look like and how many followers they have." "How did that affect your grades?" "I just didn't like hanging out with those kids, so I didn't go to class," he said. I asked, "What would help you most?" "I just want to be able to hang out with some real kids. I don't like huge crowds and I would love to be able to have more time to talk to my profs when I need to. And, I don't like being so far away from home." In the following sessions, I worked with his parents to let go of their romantic notion of Dylan graduating from their Alma Mater. I shared my mental fitness framework with them. Dylan had all of the book smarts in the world and was extremely unhappy because he wasn't socially connected. As he struggled socially, he began to isolate and lose interest in academics. Ultimately, his parents had to face the fact that what had been a good college for them, was not a good fit for Dylan.

What parent doesn't want their child to get into a good college?! Of course, we all want our kids to have the best chance possible for success and happiness in life. The problem is, as parents, we sometimes lose sight of how and where to focus our energy. Dylan's parents were convinced that he would be happy and flourish in the Ivy league atmosphere that was so magical for them. Sometimes we have to change our perspective and redefine what **"good college"** means. It could very well mean an elite school. If your child meets the criteria to get accepted into Harvard and they are excited about the opportunity, by all means, go for it! But, please don't rule out other possibilities, such as public or state universities and community colleges. If your child has struggled with grades in high school, or if money is tight, attending a community college for the first two years can be an affordable and efficient pathway to getting accepted into a four-year college.

Initially, Dylan's parents struggled with the notion of re-defining their beliefs regarding the definition of a good college. I worked to help them look at Dylan from a holistic perspective, taking into consideration his IQ and his EQ. It was clear that he had strong academic skills. There was no doubt about his intellec-tual ability, however, he had challenges socially and emotionally. He needed to have relationships with his professors, to be closer to home, and to connect socially with peers that he felt he could relate to. He did not have the emotional capacity to verbalize his needs and ended up shutting down and isolating himself. In the end, Dylan's parents were able to redefine what a good college is. They supported his decision to transfer to a smaller school closer to home that had less prestige than his other school, but a very solid engineering program nonetheless. Once his EQ needs were met, Dylan was able to return to the competent high IQ student that he had always been. He has since graduated and is happily working as an engineer for a successful company in town.

Chapter 11 Assignment: Meet with your teen and have a dis-cussion to get an idea of what a "**good college**" is for them. Ask them some questions: What are your favorite classes in school? Have you thought about a major? How do you learn best? To answer this question, you may have to prompt them to remember a specific time or setting they were in that was conducive to learning (e.g., large groups, small groups, independent study, lecture, online, close relationship with teacher). Have your child make a list of their top 10 criteria for a good college fit. Be sure to revisit this list when looking at college options.

Chapter 12:
Sleeping with the Enemy

If you're feeling overwhelmed by hearing about the struggles your iGen child is experiencing in reading this book, imagine how they are feeling. Think about all of the information coming to them through electronic devices as their brains mature and their identities develop! As parents, we are well aware that something is wrong when our kids act out, scream at us, or get into trouble in the community. When our kids sit quietly in a room with an electronic device, it is easy to assume everything is OK. What we have not been aware of, however, is that the true enemy is right under our noses and in our children's bedrooms. Our iGen kids are physically safer due to isolation from each other as a result of wireless devices, but much more mentally fragile and unprepared to take on the rigors of college life. A lot of parents who come to me have a hard time solving this problem because they aren't aware of how pervasive it is. Have you ever seen a child's reaction when they lose their cellphone or you try to take it away from them? When I chat with parents about how much time and energy it will take to unwire their child and get them on the road to mental fitness for success in college, they are surprised. They have been making some well-meaning attempts with their kids, but due to being busy themselves, have not been able to break through. I have given you a framework for success in this book and it works. What you need to know is that it takes practice and persistence to gain competence in applying these steps to real life. In the coaching field, we talk about four stages of competence:

Stage I - Unconscious Incompetence: In this initial stage, we are misdirected in our efforts to help our kids succeed in school and unaware of it; like the well-meaning "type triple A" dad in chapter 11 who tried to take over his son's college application process.

Stage II - Conscious Incompetence: We are consciously aware that we are struggling to help our kids succeed in school. Upon reflection, in Chapter 9, Amy's mother realized that what she had been doing to help her daughter was not working.

Stage III - Conscious Competence: We are consciously aware that we are helping our child succeed in school. After 6 months of working with Christopher's parents in chapter 7, they became aware that their new strategies were working.

Stage IV - Unconscious Competence: We have learned to help our kids in school so well that we don't have to think about it. In chapter 11, Dylan's parents trusted the process and participated one hundred percent. We ended after only a few weeks because they had integrated the skills to a point where they didn't have to think about what they were doing. It just came naturally.

What would it be like to learn how to guide your child to success in school so well, that it becomes as natural as breathing? All children deserve an opportunity to get in a position in life where they are doing what they were born to do. And nothing pains me more than to see parents stuck. It is easy for us to feel like a failure when our kids are struggling. We can get caught up in comparing ourselves to other parents whose kids seem to be doing better than ours. And it hurts us to see our kids so sad and withdrawn, wired up with TV, cellphones, and computers in their rooms with the door closed. It can be very anxiety-producing when we don't know if our kids are depressed, or if they could potentially do something to harm themselves. And the thought of seeing them get passed up by their peers is painful. As parents, all we really want is a happy, healthy child, with the skills to take on the world and succeed in college and career.

One of my favorite client memories is a celebration I had with a mother and her daughter, with whom I had worked for quite some time. Mary had been struggling notoriously in school. We worked through all kinds of distractions and teen stressors. Her mother hung in like a trooper. I got a phone call one day from Mom, ecstatic about receiving news that her daughter had been accepted into the University of Minnesota. We had a party in my office. To see the look on Mary's face! Her world had expanded. Mom's life opened up as well—"I have more time for self-care and now we are thinking about doing some traveling." She cheerfully reported that her relationship with her husband had been improving due to much less stress in the house.

Parents, I wish you well on your journey with your child on the road to getting into a good college. You have demonstrated your commitment. You've got this! Remember your skills, breathe, you're almost there, you are going to be so happy!

Chapter 13: Conclusion

"Only the educated are free."
— Epictetus

By nature, teen years can be quite turbulent as our kids are growing, developing, and seeking to discover who they are. Today's teens, however, are experiencing some unique struggles that we need to look at from a societal perspective. The truth is that our teens and young adults, who have been referred to in this book as the "iGen" or internet generation, are experiencing historically high levels of mental health problems that have been showing up in high schools and on college campuses all over the world. "iGen" refers to kids born after 1995, who have grown up with the internet and other forms of wireless technology. There is very strong evidence that this exposure has resulted in significant delays in developing the social and emotional skills necessary to maintain mental fitness and succeed in school. Through my experience as a psychologist and coach, I have learned that if something is caused by an environmental factor, there is always an action we can take to remedy it. That's good news! Parents, if your child is battling to get good grades and get into a good college, there is a solution.

The process I have outlined is easy to follow, however, it takes commitment and stick-to-itiveness. In chapter 1, I highlighted the importance of getting started on the mental fitness process as soon as possible to ensure your child is ready to take on the rigors of college life. In chapter 2, I shared stories of my own personal struggles with college, and how I solved the problem. Chapter 3 underscores the importance of foundational and emotional intelligence skills. In chapter 4, we did some exploration to help you become clear, not only about concerns for your child, but also hopes and dreams. In chapter 5, I provided several examples of parenting styles and encouraged you to examine the connection between how you were parented and how you are currently parenting your child. In chapter 6, I discussed pressing problems unique to iGen kids, such as electronics and social media, bullying, loneliness, the vaping epidemic, peer pressure, teen suicide, and the sharp increase in depression and anxiety. Chapter 7 was about learning how to clean the slate with your child in order to design a strong working alliance as you moved into the mental fitness process. In chapter 8, I reviewed the foundational skills of time management, sleep hygiene, nutrition, and physical activity to help you create sustainable structures with your child to keep them on track. In the heart of the book chapter 9, I went into great detail to illuminate the importance of infusing self-awareness, social skills, and empathy to help your child succeed in school and get into a good college. Chapter 10 taught you skills for building confidence and gave you a template for setting goals. The last step, in chapter 10, "Putting it all Together," assisted you in applying these concepts towards the college application process. Finally, in chapter 12, I emphasized that getting your child into a good college may not be as hard as you think.

My hope is that, in reading this book, you feel optimistic and are armed with tools and strategies to help your child succeed in school and life. It has been an honor for me to be on this journey with you, and if I can assist you in any way, please feel free to reach out.

Acknowledgments

Firstly, my thanks go to MarDee Rosen Hall for her contributions to this book. MarDee joined *David Hoy & Associates* 23 years ago as a psychologist working with teens and families. I immediately sensed we were like-minded, sharing an intense passion to help people improve the quality of their lives. What I didn't know back then is that I not only had a like-minded colleague, but also a brilliant clinician and a super-smart understated leader who would go on to become the wind beneath our wings. As Clinical Director and a lead administrator, MarDee has helped to take us from a small private practice to a company of 100 high caliber employees having a profound impact on the health of families and children. In a similar fashion, she also contributed by joining me when I was struggling and assisting me with editing and developing the stories within the mental fitness framework presented in this book. I am grateful and very fortunate to have a friend and colleague with whom I can work so easily and freely. I look forward to more creation!

Again, to my wife of 31 years, Sandy, who has supported me unconditionally in all of my endeavors, including this one. Sandy has been our CFO and controller for 22 years. As a lead administrator, she has helped keep us safe and strong and has been a huge part of shaping a culture of generativity. I also wish to thank our lead administrators Kathy Wolfbauer and Nicole Recke for their critical support roles that enable us to provide high-quality care.

I would like to acknowledge my children, Sammy, Maddie, and David. I love you so much! Thank you for your input in this book and helping with focus groups. Thanks to your friends and acquaintances who participated and gave us very valuable feedback. Thanks always for your love and support. You are my treasures!

I also thank my friend and fraternity brother John Gabos, founder and president of *Myiceberg, Coaching and Mentoring Services*, whose passion for helping people and infectious energy were a large part of my impetus for writing this book. I look forward to our continued collaboration! I would also like to acknowledge Tina Gabos of *Myiceberg* for her diligent work collecting and evaluating research pertinent to teen mental health. I am also grateful to Paulina Gabos, who assisted in research, surveys, focus group questions, and execution. I wish you well in your budding career in the field of psychology.

Lastly, I would like to thank the *Author Incubator* for giving me a formula and a jumpstart for a book that I sincerely hope makes a difference.

About the Author

Dr. David Hoy is a licensed psychologist and a certified professional coach. He is the founder and Executive Director of *David Hoy & Associates*, a Minnesota-based Clinic of Counseling, Psychological, and Coaching Services. In its humble beginnings, *DH&A* started out in 1997 with just a handful of clients. The company has since grown to include 100 practitioners and administrative staff providing services to adults, children, and families throughout the twin cities and greater metropolitan area. Dr. Hoy earned his PhD in education with a specialization in training and performance improvement from Capella University. He holds a master's degree in counseling and psychology from

St. Mary's University and a bachelor's degree in speech and communication from the University of Minnesota. Dr. Hoy has been able to integrate his education and work experience to create a dynamic coaching process that empowers teens and young adults to take charge of their education and careers. As a consultant, he was recently featured in the *Minneapolis St. Paul Magazine* in an article entitled, *"How Minnesota Is Tackling Teen Mental Health."* David believes strongly in holistic approaches to achieving overall health and well-being. He has run 24 full-distance marathons and has since become an avid bicycle enthusiast. David strives to create a mindfulness culture at work. To this end, he hires yoga instructors who provide classes three times per week for employees. David lives in Plymouth, Minnesota, with his wife, youngest son, Lucy the dog, and Goldie the cat. He has two daughters who have recently graduated from college and launched successfully.

Thanks for reading

Remember, you don't have to do this alone. There are numerous resources and people to help. If you would like my assistance, contact me at david@davidhoy.com and we can set up a free consult to see if my program is a fit for you.

Website:
http://davidhoy.com/
Instagram:
https://www.instagram.com/davidhoyandassociates/
or the username is: davidhoyandassociates
Facebook:
https://www.facebook.com/DavidHoyandAssociates/

Selected Resources

Anderson, K. (2018). American College Health Association Survey-2014. Retrieved from http://healthyhabts.com/2018/09/21/one-third-of-first-year-college-students-report-mental-health-issues/

Arjocu, F. (2009). Mirror Neurons Part 1. https://www.youtube.com/watch?v=XzMqPYfeA-s

Azar, A. (2018). Surgeon General Warns Youth Vaping Is Now An 'Epidemic.' Retrieved from https://www.npr.org/sections/health-shots/2018/12/18/677755266/surgeon-general-warns-youth-vaping-is-now-an-epidemic

Bakalar, N. (2015). How Much Junk Food Do Teenagers Eat?. *New York Times*. Retrieved from https://www.nytimes.com/2015/09/22/health/how-much-junk-food-do-teenagers-eat.html

Bandura, A. (1977). Self-efficacy: Toward a unifying theory of behavioral change. *Psychological Review, 84*, 191-215. doi:10.1037/0033-295X.84.2.191

Bandura, A. (1986). *Social foundations of thought and action: A social cognitive approach.* Englewood Cliffs, NJ: Prentice Hall.

Baumrind, D. (2019). Diana Baumrind's 3 Parenting Styles: Get a Full Understanding of the 3 Archetypal Parents. Retrieved from https://www.positive-parenting-ally.com/3-parenting-styles.html

Buettner, D. (2017). *The Blue Zones of Happiness: Lessons From The World's Happiest People.* Washington, D.C.: National Geographic.

CASEL. (2017). Promoting Positive Youth Development Through School-Based Social and Emotional Learning Interventions: A Meta-Analysis of Follow-up Effects. Retrieved from https://casel.org/2017-meta-analysis/

Centers for Disease Control. (2000-2016). US Suicide Rates % Change: Comparison of Most Digitally Connected Generation 2000-2016. CDC data.

CDC. (2019). Mental Health. https://www.cdc.gov/childrensmental-health/data.html

Center for Generational Kinetics. (2016). An Intro To Generations. Retrieved from https://genhq.com/faq-info-about-generations/

College On Line Prep. (2019). Retrieved from http://static.square-space.com/static/527cc9ffe4b06105448def23/t/5390d40ee-4b021878060633e/1402000398123/CEG-College-Prep.pdf

Duckworth, A., Taxer, J., Winkler, L-W., Galla, B., & Gross, J. (2019). Self-Control and Academic Achievement. *Annual Review of Clinical Psychology, 70.* 373-399. Retrieved from https://doi.org/10.1146//annurev-psych-101418-103230

Goleman, D. (1995). *Emotional intelligence: Why it can matter more than IQ.* New York: Bantam Books. (6th ed).

Goleman, D. (2006). *Social intelligence: The new science of human relationships.* New York: Bantam Books.

Harris, R. (2015). Got Water, Most Kids, Teens Don't Drink Enough. Retrieved from https://www.npr.org/sections/health-shots/2015/06/11/413674246/got-water-most-kids-teens-dont-drink-enough

Heffernan, L. (2019). Grown and Flown. *Web Site*. Retrieved from https://grownandflown.com/grown-and-flown-about-us/

Heidi, M. (2019). *The loneliness Epidemic*. In *Mental Health: A New Understanding*. Time Magazine.

Hogue, D. (2019). Act to offer section retakes, online test in 2020. *Minneapolis Star and Tribune*. Retrieved from https://www.newstribune.com/news/local/story/2019/oct/13/act-to-offer-section-retakes-online-test-in-2020/799502/

Howard, J. (2019). Pediatricians Endorse Weight Loss Surgery For Severely Obese Kids And Teens: 'It Changed My Life.' Retrieved from https://www.cnn.com/2019/10/27/health/weight-loss-surgery-kids-teens-pediatrics-study/index.html

Knispel, U. (2018). Thirteen Signs Your Teen May Have An Eating Disorder. Retrieved from https://www.futurity.org/13-signs-of-eating-disorders-teens-1774822/

Lardieri, A. (2018). Study: Teens Exposed To More Junk Food Ads Eat More Junk Food. Retrieved from https://www.usnews.com/news/health-care-news/articles/2018-05-22/study-teens-exposed-to-more-junk-food-ads-eat-more-junk-food

Maslow, A. H. (1973). A theory of human motivation. In R. J. Lowry (Ed.), *Dominance, self-esteem, and self-actualization: Germinal papers of H. A. Maslow* (pp. 157-173). Belmont, CA: Wadsworth.

Newport Academy. (2017). *The Scary Truth Behind Teen Eating Disorders: Causes, Effects, and Statistics*. Retrieved from https://www.newportacademy.com/resources/mental-health/scary-truth-teen-eating-disorders/

Pew Research Center. (2019), Mobile Phone Ownership Over Time. Retrieved from https://www.pewresearch.org/internet/fact-sheet/mobile/

Reilly, K., & Heid, M. (2019). *Depression on Campus.* In *Mental Health: A New Understanding.* Time Magazine.

Richter, R. (2015). Among Teens, Sleep Deprivation an Epidemic. Retrieved from https://med.stanford.edu/news/all-news/2015/10/among-teens-sleep-deprivation-an-epidemic.html

Sandoiu, A. (2019). Teens Get as Much Exercise As 60-Year-Olds, Study Shows. Retrieved from https://www.medicalnewstoday.com/articles/317975.php

Sears, W. (2019). Breakfasts to Improve Performance. Retrieved from https://www.askdrsears.com/topics/feeding-eating/family-nutrition/brain-foods/brainy-breakfasts-improve-school-and-work-performance

Siegal, D. *The Pruning Process in the Adolescent Brain.* Retrieved from

https://www.kidsinthehouse.com/teenager/health-and-development/brain-development/pruning-process-adolescent-brain

Smith, K. (2019). Common Triggers of Teen Stress. Retrieved from https://www.psycom.net/common-triggers-teen-stress/

Staff Writer. (2018). Can Exercise Boost Your GPA? California College of San Diego. Retrieved from https://www.cc-sd.edu/blog/can-exercise-boost-your-gpa-2

Stein, S., Book, H., Kanoy, K. (2013). *The Student Edge; Emotional Intelligence and Your Personal and Academic Success,* John Wiley and Sons, Inc.

Can Exercise Boost Your GPA?. (2018). California College of San Diego. Retrieved from https://www.cc-sd.edu/blog/can-exercise-boost-your-gpa-2 https:www.verywellhealth.com/how-much-exercise-does-your-teen-really-need-2611242

The Conversation, Teens Who Meet Up With Their Friends Almost Every Day. (n.d.) Monitoring the Future Get the Data.

The Conversation, Teen Loneliness Rates. (n.d.). Monitoring the Future Get the Data.

Twenge, J. M. (2017). *iGen: Why today's super-connected kids are growing up less rebellious, more tolerant, less happy, and completely unprepared for adulthood (and what this means for the rest of us)*. New York, NY: Atria Books.

USDA Replaces Food Pyramid With 'My Plate' In Hopes To Promote Healthier Eating. (2011). The Washington Post. Retrieved from ttps://www.washingtonpost.com/national/usda-replaces-food-pyramid-with-myplate-in-hopes-to-promote-healthier-eating/2011/06/02/AGRE16HH_story.html

Made in the USA
Columbia, SC
07 March 2020